PRESENTED BY

L. L. Owens
1986

THE FACE OF ROBERT E. LEE

in Life and in Legend

BY

ROY MEREDITH

REVISED EDITION

ILLUSTRATED

THE FAIRFAX PRESS
NEW YORK

Other books by Roy Meredith

Mr. Lincoln's Camera Man: Mathew B. Brady
The Face of Robert E. Lee
Mr. Lincoln's Contemporaries
The American Wars
Storm over Sumter
This Was Andersonville
Mr. Lincoln's General: U. S. Grant
Mr. Lincoln's Military Railroads (with Arthur Meredith, Jr.)
The World of Mathew Brady
Portrait of an Era (To be published Spring, 1981)

Copyright © MCMXLVII, MCMLXXXI by Roy Meredith
All rights reserved.

This edition is published by The Fairfax Press,
distributed by Crown Publishers, Inc.,
by arrangement with Roy Meredith.
a b c d e f g h
FAIRFAX 1981 EDITION

Manufactured in the United States of America

Library of Congress Cataloging in Publication Data

Meredith, Roy, 1908–
    The face of Robert E. Lee in life and in legend.

    1. Lee, Robert E. (Robert Edward), 1807–1870—
Portraits, caricatures, etc.   2. Generals—United
States—Portraits.   I. Title.
E467.1.L4M5   1981   973.7'3'0924   [B]   81-1073
ISBN 0-517-33637-5   AACR2

CONTENTS AND LIST OF ILLUSTRATIONS

FROM THE LEGEND

ACKNOWLEDGMENTS

THE AUTHOR is deeply aware of his debt to many contributors for their wholehearted search through archives and family records for facts, photographs, and pictures, which when brought together made possible this story of the visual representations of Robert E. Lee.

The compiling of this material presented a formidable task until the writer learned the true extent of Southern helpfulness. Without friendly counsel and friendly aid, it would have been a difficult task indeed.

I am grateful to Miss India Thomas, House Regent of the Confederate Museum, Richmond, for supplying many of the pictures and for her manifold courtesies; to Mrs. Ralph Catterall, Curator of Documents of the Valentine Museum in Richmond, for the kind provision of numerous pictures and important background material on Edward V. Valentine and his work with General Lee; to Mrs. Ferguson Carey, Historian General of the United Daughters of the Confederacy, for encouragement in this undertaking; to Mrs. George Coleman for many helpful suggestions; to Mrs. Blair Stringfellow for the use of the photograph belonging to her family; to Dr. Douglas Southall Freeman, biographer of Robert E. Lee, for constructive ideas and for a wealth of information in *R. E. Lee,* his definitive Life of this book's subject; to the Reverend Clayton Torrence, Secretary of the Virginia Historical Society, for his cooperation in supplying pictures and data from the collection of the Society; to Colonel Catesby ap Catesby Jones, of the Virginia Historical Society, for notable suggestions; to Mr. A. L. Dementi for providing many pictures; to Mr. Huestis Cook, son of the famous Confederate photographer, George Cook, for some rare prints of General Lee; to Dr. Hutchinson W. Morrison for a very rare daguerreotype, unfortunately too reticulated to be used; to Mr. Alexander H. Sands, Vice President of the Virginia Historical Society, for supplying a rare picture; to Mr. Van Dyk Mac Bride; to Mr. Carl E. Dorr; to Mr. John Jennings, Librarian of William and Mary College; to Mr. Walter Hopkins, Adjutant General, Sons of Confederate Veterans; to Mr. James Cogar, Curator of Books, Colonial Williamsburg; to Dr. and Mrs. Leslie Campbell; to Dr. J. H. Eckenrode, Director of Archæology, Virginia Conservation Commission; to Miss Julia Sully, historian; to Mr. Harry Harris; to Miss Frances Lichten; to Mr. Clifford Dowdey, author of *Experiment in Rebellion,* for many helpful efforts in behalf of this project.

To Miss Rose M. E. MacDonald I am grateful for the light shed by her biográphical study, *Mrs. R. E. Lee,* in the obscurity which has surrounded the first portrait of Robert E. Lee. To the Lee Museum of Lexington, and to the Administration of Washington and Lee University go my special thanks, notably to the president, Dr. Francis P. Gaines, to Mr. E. S. Mattingly, the treasurer, and to Miss Helen Webster, the assistant treasurer. Help from the Museum and Society historical collections in Richmond has already been acknowledged. In addition a debt is owed to the Metropolitan Museum of Art in New York, the Pennsylvania Academy of the Fine Arts in Philadelphia, the Public Library of Galena, Illinois, the City of Dallas, Texas, and the Dallas Chamber of Commerce. Miss Jean Fisher and Miss Harriet Cohn have assisted in the assembling of many important details.

R. M.

FOREWORD TO THE 1981 EDITION

I first proposed *The Face of Robert E. Lee* to my friend, the late Maxwell E. Perkins, senior editor of Charles Scribner's Sons, in 1946, following the publication of *Mr. Lincoln's Camera Man: Mathew B. Brady,* and the book was published in 1947.

The premise of the book was to provide an intellectual complement of photographic and artistic studies of the Confederacy's greatest soldier made during his lifetime. I owned a number of authentic photographs of General Lee, taken by Mathew Brady, the world-renowned portrait photographer, but the small number of actual photographs of Lee then in existence didn't accord with Lee's military eminence, North or South. On the other hand, an infinite number of romanticized engravings, lithographs, and aquatints were plentiful—enough to fill several books. But these, for the most part, placed Lee in imaginary situations and were largely inaccurate.

At the time, a diligent search for authentic photographs and artistic representations, taken from life, revealed a goodly number of important pictures of General Lee hitherto unknown. These, coupled with the best of the legendary, romanticized illustrations, formed the basis of the book and presented a fairly rounded iconographic study of the revered commander of the Army of Northern Virginia. To this I have added new subject matter and new illustrations.

Today, Robert E. Lee is surrounded in persistent legend, and the War of the Southern Confederacy is still regarded as "the last of the romantic wars," an observation made some years ago by the late Fletcher Pratt. He was partially right; an irresistible romantic notion still lingers over our old "family war." To many young soldiers of the South in 1861, the war was an exciting adventure, and they saw themselves as knights in shining armor going forth to do battle for the Cause.

"JEB" Stuart, Wade Hampton, Major John Pelham, and P. T. G. Beauregard were among the South's romantic military figures; but Robert E. Lee became the most prominent of them all—the South's leading cavalier hero, even more so than "Stonewall" Jackson.

The Northern soldiers had no such romantic notions. To them the war was "an organized bore," as described by Captain Oliver Wendell Holmes, who saw action in most of the major battles. The harsh truth is, however, that the Civil War was one of the bloodiest, most desperately-fought conflicts in all U. S. history. There was nothing that could remotely be called "romantic" about the sanguinary fighting—in such terrifying battles as Antietam, Fredericksburg, or Gettysburg—that destroyed the lives of thousands of young soldiers, sometimes in a single day.

The illustrations portray Lee as the handsome, romantic soldier who led the Southern armies in that tragic war of long ago, and the illustrations are truthful. Lee's personal gallantry, impeccable character, and soldierly qualities earned him that reputation and sobriquet, and rightfully so. His like, as a soldier and man, will never be seen again.

It is the author's hope that the revisions and addition of five, striking, new illustrations will enhance and broaden the scope of the original edition.

ROY MEREDITH
November 1, 1980

FROM THE LIFE

NO ATTEMPT is made here to tell the story of the life of Robert E. Lee in pictures, though wherever chronology can be established, that natural order is followed.

The material of this first section derives from Lee in person; he was its direct visual inspiration. Here is his image on the retina of the artist or his reflection on the eye of the camera. Three times in his life Lee sat to painters of portraits. Another portrait seems to have been begun from life. He was daguerreotyped twice, possibly three times. There is one tintype, though it seems not to be an original. As the art of photography expanded, his likeness was recorded more frequently. From the years of the war there are eight indubitable original photographs, and many variants on these. There is an artist's quick sketch of him as he appeared in the field. Another artist's portrayal of one of Lee's moments of deep personal emotion is believed to have been based on the detailed observation of an eye-witness or perhaps of several, and so is included. In the five years of Lee's life after the war the camera found him often—there are at least 23 distinct subjects, originals which cannot be called into question. The plastic art, the art of the sculptor, handed down four authentic examples. Included in this record of the actual, there is one exception, a recent work of reconstruction; but it is a synthesis so admirable that it deserves a special status.

Here, then, is Lee as he was in life, in so far as the likenesses have been preserved. There were other photographs, but not even copies of them have survived. And in those days as now, photographers beguiled their clients by artful retouching. Many of the photographs that Lee himself or his family gave out in response to the hundreds of requests were far from the reality; many of the signs of age and bodily wear had been touched away. Here we are concerned only with the authentic, the unretouched originals. We want to know how Lee really looked.

The record has been further confused by the imitative arts. Original negatives were retouched, then rephotographed, perhaps retouched and rephotographed again. Lithographs that were based on photographs would be photographed in turn, and the results would be circulated as original photographs. It has been the aim to show where all these dubious and generally unconvincing subjects have their source.

Until the twentieth century brought the perfecting of the photo-engraving process, readers of newspapers and magazines could see a reasonable facsimile of a photograph only in the form of a steel engraving or a wood engraving, executed by a craftsman. Some of these engravings are included here, even though many of them went wide of the mark. They are all that millions of Lee's contemporaries, and millions of readers for several decades after his death, ever knew; it is the way they thought he looked.

Again, these pictures and their captions do not try to tell the story of the life of Robert E. Lee. Whenever it has been possible to date a photograph or a painting, exactly or even approximately, the accompanying text sets forth what is known about the circumstances of its making and the conditions of his life which formed its background. Sometimes the author presents what he feels is reasonable conjecture.

THE FIRST PORTRAIT

THE HISTORY of the pictures and photographs of Robert E. Lee begins with a portrait in oils. Though it was long assigned to the year 1831, examination of the letters of Mrs. Lee has recently disclosed that it was painted in 1838, when Lee was thirty-one. The portrait had been obscurely ascribed to "Benjamin West, Jr.," but Mrs. Lee's letters reveal also that the painter was William E. West, who evidently had returned from his successes in Europe a year or two earlier than has been generally supposed.

We see Lee here in the full-dress uniform of a Lieutenant of Engineers of the United States Army, wearing the side whiskers that were then the fashion. He was already the father of two sons and a daughter. Mrs. Lee had been through an alarming illness, and her husband, separated from his family for months at a time, had known deep worry and a growing sense of frustration. In this month of March 1838, however, he was full of reassurance, for the loneliness and home-sickness he had endured in St. Louis in the preceding summer and autumn were not to be repeated. After a winter in Arlington and Washington he was on his way back to St. Louis to resume his work as superintending engineer for St. Louis harbor and the upper Mississippi and Missouri rivers, but this time his wife and three children were with him.

On their way to take a west-bound river steamer at Pittsburgh, they stopped off in Baltimore, where lived Lee's sister, Mrs. William Louis Marshall. They had gone there by way of the new Baltimore and Ohio railroad, which then ran only as far as Frederick. From Baltimore, Mrs. Lee wrote to her mother, Mrs. George Washington Parke Custis, that she had persuaded her husband to sit for his portrait, and that it had been painted "by William E. West & his picture is a very fine likeness & a fine painting." She wrote further that Lee was urging her to sit also, but that she preferred to have her portrait done by Sully. Before the letter was posted, however, she added that she had, after all, "determined to sit for my picture & Robert has agreed to remain till Monday week." Mrs. Custis must already have known that a portrait was in progress, for Lee himself had written to his mother-in-law at Arlington asking her to send him his epaulets, "as Mary has gotten around me and persuaded me to have my portrait painted by a young American artist . . . William E. West." (West in reality was then fifty, nineteen years older than Lee.)

The two portraits apparently were sent to Arlington, for Mrs. Custis, evidently somewhat critical at first, wrote to her daughter in St. Louis that she was now beginning to like them better. In reply Mrs. Lee confessed: "I did not like either of them altogether, but I had only a moment to look at them after they were finished. You must take the opinion of strangers generally as you are too partial a judge."*

---

*The brief excerpts from Mrs. Lee's letters are quoted from Rose Mortimer Ellzey MacDonald's informing biographical study, *Mrs. Robert E. Lee,* published by Ginn and Co., 1939.

To our eyes the portrait seems the perfect embodiment of the man whom his contemporaries have pictured for us in words. A few months earlier, Lee had said goodbye in Washington to a young engineer who had been his friend and assistant in St. Louis, Second Lieutenant Montgomery C. Meigs, later to be quartermaster-general of the Union Army during the War Between the States. In after years, Meigs described Lee as he was in 1838: a man "in the vigor of youthful strength, with a noble and commanding presence, and an admirable, graceful and athletic figure. He was one with whom nobody ever wished or ventured to take a liberty, though kind and generous to all his subordinates, admired by all women, and respected by all men. He was the model of a soldier and the beau ideal of a Christian man."

From this countenance those qualities look out which Lee's biographer, Douglas Southall Freeman ascribes to the young officer. "He was five feet, ten and a half inches in height," writes Dr. Freeman, "with brown eyes that sometimes seemed black. His hair was ebon and abundant, with a wave that a woman might have envied. There was dignity in his open bearing, and his manners were considerate and ingratiating. He had candor, tact, and good humor. The self control he had learned from his mother was his in larger measure. . . . It was easy for him to win and hold the friendship of other people."

After the death of Mrs. Lee, the portrait became the property of G. W. C. Lee, and remained at Washington and Lee University during Custis Lee's long presidency, eventually coming into the possession of the widow of Colonel Robert E. Lee, who was a son of W. H. F. Lee and a grandson of Robert E. Lee. The background is a deep brownish maroon; the uniform is a very dark blue, almost black, with epaulets, collar insignia and buttons in gold. Hair and side whiskers are a dark brown. Although the surface of the canvas has checked badly, as the unretouched photograph indicates, the face has not been seriously impaired.

A word of dissent from this portrait as a likeness came from E. V. Valentine. The sculptor, who took Lee's measurements in 1870 in preparation for modeling a head of him, said that his lips were not so full as the West painting showed them. Lee was then heavily bearded, and observation must have been difficult. Moreover he was sixty-three, and the passing of thirty-two years full of austerities might well have wrought a change in his mouth.

WAS THIS LEE AT THIRTY-EIGHT?

THIS MAY BE ROBERT E. LEE. Although the author believes it to be the result of Lee's first encounter with the very new art of daguerreotypy, it can be offered only tentatively. There is no way of authenticating this photographic copy of a daguerreotype, which is included in the Lee file of the Virginia Historical Society but is not vouched for by the Society. H. M. Miley, Lexington photographer in the days of Lee's presidency of Washington College, said that in 1867 one of R. E. Lee's daughters brought the daguerreotype to him to be copied. The daguerreotype itself has been lost. That is all we know.

The suggestion is put forward here that this shows a daguerreotype of Robert E. Lee and his son "Rooney," taken in New York in the early autumn of 1845, quite possibly in the studio that Mathew B. Brady had opened on the corner of Broadway and Fulton Street in 1844. The Lees were then living at Fort Hamilton, on The Narrows of New York harbor. Custis had been sent back to Virginia for his schooling, and it would have been natural for Lee and his second son, now turned eight, to have visited nearby New York together. Perhaps on the spur of the moment, perhaps to surprise Mrs. Lee, they stopped in at "Brady's Daguerrian Miniature Gallery." Lee would then have been thirty-eight, an age which accords with his appearance here. Hair and whiskers, eyes, nose and lips seem to be his. We know that he was still wearing side whiskers as late as October of 1843, for when his third son was born he wrote to a friend: "He has a fine long nose like his father, but no whiskers." Probably the side whiskers survived until the departure for the Mexican War. The boy has Robert E. Lee's highly distinctive ear, while his mouth resembles Mrs. Lee's. Both details seem to have been true of "Rooney."

Lee's third son, Robert Edward, has been quoted on page 22 of this volume as deploring the fact that because his father so hated having to sit for his portrait, no photograph or painting ever showed the "sweetness of disposition" that was the natural expression of his mouth. Here surely is one that does. Lee has not yet learned to dislike having his picture taken; here he is wholly unselfconscious, interested in something new, amiably alert and cooperative.

All this is conjecture. This picture probably can never be authenticated. But if the reader of this book, after he has studied all the pictures of Lee as he was in life, will return to this daguerreotype he may join the writer in his conviction that this is a familiar face.

An argument in the negative is the unlikelihood that this picture would have been lost to the sight and memory of all of Lee's family, after one of his daughters had gone to the trouble of having it copied. It is unlikely too that Brady would have forgotten about this daguerreotype if it had been of his making. He himself vaguely said he had known Lee "since the Mexican War, when he was on General Scott's staff"—an assignment which began for Lee in January of 1847, but ended two or perhaps three years before Brady's first known daguerreotype of Lee. Some other early photographer may have made it. The puzzle remains.

THE FIRST DAGUERREOTYPE

THE FIRST fully authenticated photograph of Lee is believed to have been made shortly before the outbreak of the war with Mexico. Genuine though the likeness is, what one sees here is not the original, a daguerreotype which has not survived. Shown on the facing page is a photograph of that daguerreotype, a copy made by Boude and Miley of Lexington, Virginia, some time in the late fifties after the wet plate had come into prominence. The same photographers may also have made the original daguerreotype, although there is no record of Lee's having visited Lexington in those years.

Vignetted to disclose only head and shoulders, as was the custom of photographers in that era, this copy shows Lee in the uniform of a Captain of Engineers. With changing fashion the side whiskers have disappeared and a moustache has been added. He still wears his hair long and full over the temples, as in fact he did throughout his life, and it is worth noting that in these years he parted his hair on the right side.

The reader of this volume will be aware of the close resemblance of this copy of a daguerreotype to the later daguerreotype shown on page 21. The possibility exists that what is shown opposite is merely a retouched copy of the other. The Brady daguerreotype, however, discloses a more mature man, and the present subject can be offered with reasonable assurance as genuine. Lee's autograph cannot be taken as absolute evidence of authenticity, since it would have been simple for a photographer to incorporate an autograph when making a new negative.

AFTER THE MEXICAN WAR

SHORTLY AFTER Mathew B. Brady opened his photographic gallery in Washington in the year 1850, he made this original daguerreotype of Lee in civilian dress. Colonel Lee was then in charge of the construction of the military defenses of the port of Baltimore, notably the building of Fort Carroll, a task that occupied him until he became superintendent of the United States Military Academy in 1852. He had been brevet Colonel since August of 1848, having been advanced in rank three times for distinguished service in the war with Mexico. When this daguerreotype was taken he was forty-three or forty-four, and we have his own word for it that there were furrows in his face and white hairs in his head. Returning from the war at the end of June 1848, after almost two years' separation from his family, he wrote to his brother, Smith Lee, that his children stared fascinated at these new signs of age in him.

This daguerreotype dates definitely from 1850 or 1851. Like the earlier one, it was later to be widely copied and elaborated—a practice begun by Brady himself when the advent of the wet plate in 1856 made prints on paper possible. In this original, for later reference note in the lower right corner that Lee's white-gloved hands are crossed in his lap and that one of them holds his top hat.

THE SECOND PORTRAIT

ON THE FIRST DAY of September of 1852 Colonel Lee returned somewhat unwillingly to the West Point from which he had been graduated twenty-three years earlier. His reluctance was due to the fact that he was now to be ninth superintendent of the United States Military Academy, and he felt himself inadequate for a post "requiring more skill and more experience than I command." He had asked, in fact, that the War Department reconsider the appointment, only to have the order confirmed. There must have been consolation in the fact that he would again be near his eldest son Custis, who was still a cadet at The Point, and for three or four years he would have his family with him, established in a handsome house at the centre of a pleasant social life.

His third son, Robert Edward, was nearly nine at the time the move to West Point was made, old enough to begin to be aware of the life about him and to retain his observations and impressions. More than a half century later he published his invaluable memoir, *Recollections and Letters of General Robert E. Lee,* and that book is our main source of information on the portrait shown opposite, a portrait painted by Robert W. Weir, who spent forty-two years as instructor and professor of drawing at the Academy. The new superintendent liked to talk to Weir, and is said to have visited his house often.

"At this time," the younger Lee wrote, in apparent reference to the year 1853, "my father's family and friends persuaded him to allow R. S. [R. W.] Weir, Professor of Painting and Drawing at the Academy, to paint his portrait. As far as I remember, there was only one sitting, and the artist had to finish it from memory or from the glimpses he obtained of his subject in the regular course of their daily lives at 'The Point.' The picture shows my father in the undress uniform of a Colonel of Engineers, and many think it a very good likeness. To me, the expression of strength peculiar to his face is wanting, and the mouth fails to portray that sweetness of disposition so characteristic of his countenance. Still it was like him at that time. My father never could bear to have his picture taken, and there are no likenesses of him that really give his sweet expression. Sitting for a picture was such a serious business with him that he never could 'look pleasant'."

The son's recollection serves to explain a suggestion of posturing in this portrait, something unfamiliar in its quality: it does not seem like Lee. With only one sitting on which to base his study, Weir was striving to capture an impression, trying for freedom of style and at the same time to avoid the veil of grave reserve that came over the face of a man who "never could bear to have his picture taken."

LEE AT WEST POINT

HERE, AMONG the photographs and paintings that derive directly from Lee as he was in life, is a reconstruction, admitted into this section of the present volume because it expresses so satisfying a concept of what Lee must have looked like when war was imminent and his historical moment was near. Ernest L. Ipsen painted this three-quarter lifesize portrait in 1931, after what must have been the closest study of the authentic likenesses and of all recorded descriptions of Lee by his contemporaries. From them he achieved an impressive synthesis. The portrait bears the inscription "Robert E. Lee, Colonel of Engineers, U. S. A.—Superintendent."

Lee may very well have looked remarkably like the man who stands here when, in 1855, he turned over the superintendency of the Academy to his successor. To a beholder he must have seemed just this manner of man on an historic April day six years later, when he left Arlington forever and boarded a south-bound train at Alexandria. He was, however, no longer in uniform. Two days earlier he had resigned his colonel's commission in the United States Army, and now he was on his way to share the fate of Virginia.

Douglas Freeman quotes one of Lee's fellow travellers who observed him on the train that day and termed him "the noblest-looking man I had ever seen." Dr. Freeman gives us this picture of Lee as he was in that year of decision: "His fine large head, which had a circumference of twenty-three and one half inches, was broadly rounded, with prominent brows and temples, and was set on a short, strong neck. His hair was black with a sprinkle of gray; his short mustache was wholly black. Brown eyes that seemed black in dim light and a slightly florid complexion gave warmth and color to his grave face. . . . A massive torso rose above narrow hips, and his large hands were in contrast to very small feet. . . . His manners accorded with his person. In 1861, as always, he was the same in his bearing to men of every station, courteous, simple, and without pretense."

Although this is the concept of him that most Southerners had in mind during the early years of the war, Lee is not seen again in this now familiar pre-war phase. When the camera next found him, the war was near its crisis; he was heavily bearded and greatly changed in appearance.

WHAT THEY SAW
IN THE NORTH

I T WAS ON APRIL 22nd, 1861, in Richmond, that Lee accepted Governor Letcher's tender of the command of the military and naval forces of Virginia, with the rank of Major General, an appointment which was confirmed by the Virginia state convention next day. At once the name of Robert E. Lee leaped into prominence in the news. What did he look like? The press wanted to answer that question.

It must be borne in mind that the photo-engraving process did not reach a satisfactory stage of development until the twentieth century. In the days of the War Between the States, the public prints were able to show a reasonable likeness of a photograph only in the form of an engraving on steel or wood, painstakingly copied from it by a craftsman. Until the war was well along, the only likenesses of Lee available for engravers in the North, and for that matter in the South as well, were the photographic copies of the two daguerreotypes shown on pages 19 and 21. They explain the representations reproduced on this page and on the page opposite.

In 1861 this "photograph" of General Lee began to circulate, apparently having been issued first in Baltimore. It is obviously a reworking of the Brady daguerreotype of ten years earlier (shown on page 21). The uniform has been painted on, and the top hat to be seen in the original has been embellished with insignia and the initials V A to give a not wholly accurate representation of a Virginia militia dress hat. The whole was then rephotographed at an angle which makes the posture slightly less erect. The uniform, however, is that of the United States Army, which suggests that the "photograph" appeared at a time when the actual uniform could only be conjectured. The retouching was done somewhat clumsily, as the details of this reproduction clearly reveal. Probably Mathew B. Brady himself had his daguerreotype adapted.

THE REBEL GENERAL LEE.—[PHOTOGRAPHED BY BRADY.]

In its turn, the retouched and rephotographed daguerreotype was copied as a wood engraving. In August, 1861, it appeared in *Harper's Weekly* with the title "The Rebel General Lee," to illustrate comment on the resignation of Colonel Lee from the United States Army and his installation as Major General at the head of the military and naval forces of Virginia. Folds in the coat of the engraving correspond to those in the retouched photograph, indicating that the latter was the subject used by the engraver, A. H. Ritchie, although he lengthened the coat by the addition of another pair of buttons and eliminated the gloved hand and the dubious detail of the hat. The fact that the credit carries the words "Photographed by Brady" is evidence that Brady himself was responsible for the retouched daguerreotype.

In the early years of the war, this steel engraving was reproduced in Frank Leslie's weekly publication. The daguerreotype shown in a photographic copy on page 19 is the unmistakable source. The engraver-copyist reversed the subject and elaborated the uniform. The fact that a copy of this daguerreotype evidently was in circulation at the start of the war is added evidence that the daguerreotype had been a genuine original, antedating the one made by Brady.

THE ONLY TINTYPE OF GENERAL LEE

SOMETIME IN THE summer of 1861, when his active campaigning began, Lee stopped shaving. We know that by October of that year he was heavily bearded and greatly changed in appearance. For the nine years of life that remained to him he was to have the full gray beard that is completely identified in the American mind with the man whom a whole nation holds in veneration.

On the opposite page is a photograph of the only tintype of General Lee in existence, which was a gift to the Confederate Museum in Richmond from Mr. W. H. French, a Virginian. The date assigned to it is 1862, but visual evidence is offered on the following pages that it derives from a photograph which may have that year's date. The tintype shows the right side of his face in a three-quarters view, an aspect of him not often encountered, since photographers and portraitists usually preferred to pose him with the left side of his face the more fully exposed to the camera.

Even aside from the unaccustomed beard, this does not look quite like Lee. The strangeness is due chiefly to the fact that the tintype undoubtedly is a "retake" of a photograph in reverse, a circumstance which always subtly falsifies a subject's face. The smoothness of the hair, an unrealistic detail, is to be found in no other photograph of Lee in any phase of his life. Nor is the full modeling of the cheeks and the careful delineation of the area around the eyes characteristic of Lee, on the evidence of later pictures. The reader will further perceive, as he progresses through the succeeding photographs, that when Lee grew a beard he shifted the parting of his hair from the right side to the left, and did not again vary his practice throughout his life. It is here shown parted on the right.

GENERAL LEE IN THE FIELD

HERE UNDOUBTEDLY is the "master" photograph of this period, the common ancestor of the preceding tintype and of many other variants, all of them slightly puzzling because they are not entirely convincing.

This photograph is reputed to be the only one taken of General Lee in the field, and there is some evidence to support that idea. It is accredited to Bendann of Baltimore, a manifest impossibility. It is true that in the years of the war there were many travelling photographers representing Northern galleries. But it is unlikely that Lee would have posed for any of these men except at the special request of officers of his staff, in its turn an unlikely circumstance. His growing reluctance to allow himself to be photographed would hardly have been put aside for the benefit of a photographer known to represent Northern interests. Furthermore, if such a man, or indeed any unknown photographer, had been found wandering around headquarters even in a lull in military operations, he would have been hustled away with all despatch.

The author believes that this photograph was the work of Minnis and Cowell of Richmond, like the photograph shown on page 35, and that both were made on the same occasion, quite possibly in the field.

Special attention is directed to certain points in this picture which are common to a whole group of pictures. Note the folds and small creases in the coat, the partly unbuttoned waistcoat; they are recurring details. Note what seems to be a slightly disarranged bowtie, as if the right side had dipped lower than the left. This may be merely an effect of shadow, but it is to be found in the preceding tintype and in every one of the derivative likenesses which follow. Attention is directed also to the fact that each lapel has been held flat at the top by tucking its edge under a button. This detail is to be found in every subject and has a significance which will be explained later.

The photograph shown opposite was copied in a greater variety of forms and elaborations than any other. It was undoubtedly the first one taken after the war opened, and it became available at a time when the press and public were hungry for a contemporary likeness of General Lee. The date was probably some time in 1862.

[31]

At right is a reduction of the tintype, reversed a second time to restore its true value. At left is the foregoing photograph, reduced to the same head size and masked in order to take in the torso to the same depth only. At once the derivation of the tintype from the photograph becomes apparent. The identity in the details of dress is now conclusive.

This is a photograph of an admirably executed lithograph, clearly based on the photograph on page 31, as a comparison of details will show. The lithograph was published by Coupie et Cie of Paris, London, and Berlin and widely distributed throughout Europe in the last year of the War Between the States. This likeness in its turn probably was the basis of the so-called *cartes-de-visite* shown on the opposite page.

Now that the use of the wet plate was making photographic prints on paper readily possible, photographers were copying subjects freely in a convenient, small size and were distributing prints from these new negatives, chiefly for the sentimental possession of some interested individual. Such a *carte* was something like the modern postcard photograph. Soldiers killed in battle would have on their persons small photographic prints of some loved one; many a dead Confederate was found to be carrying one of these prints of Robert E. Lee. The two shown here were credited to Davies of Richmond; they were again rephotographed and distributed by E. & H. T. Anthony of New York City. The figure on the left is a vignetted enlargement of the figure on the right, but both appear to be retouched copies, photographed with the head in a slightly different posture, of the fine lithograph shown opposite, resembling it in the elaboration of the eyes (here touched up into a somewhat sentimentalized aspect of the tragic), and in the defined modeling of the cheeks. Skilfully done, neither copy seems quite true to the Lee shown in photographs which are undeniable originals; his natural reserve seldom allowed such an open reading of his feelings.

These card photos from the Confederacy often were crudely hand-colored.

It is obvious that A. Robin, who made this engraving, worked from the photograph shown on page 31, or from one of the *cartes* or lithographs deriving from it. The wide circulation it attained soon after the war makes it the more regrettable that he did not capture the spirit of the original more successfully. The heavy cast of features shown here was not General Lee's.

Here is shown what seems to be a *carte* photograph of another lithograph, which was based in turn on the photograph shown on page 31. This *carte* was made by Tanner and Van Ness, photographers of Lynchburg, and was captioned "The Only Picture of Lee in the Field." The persistence of this label in connection with variants of the photograph suggests again that there was foundation for the claim.

This fine *carte*, deriving either from the lithograph shown on page 32 or from the original photograph, seems more true in its expression to the genuine photographic record of Lee. Widely distributed throughout the Confederacy, it provided the central portrait in "The Military Medallion," a *montage* of individual portraits of Lee and his staff which found a place on the wall in many Southern homes. This negative gave a more erect posture to the head, an alteration which brought with it a slight change of values.

This extremely rare photograph of General Lee was made by Messrs. Minnis and Cowell of Richmond, quite possibly in the field. The author asks that it be studied in relationship to the photograph shown on page 31. He believes that this negative was made on the same occasion, *just before the other*. Being in the field, Lee had been wearing his coat of heavy winter material buttoned at the collar, and was photographed so. Then an easier, more relaxed pose was suggested. He unbuttoned his collar and turned back the lapels, even undid a button or two of his waistcoat. The lapels resisting their new position, Lee had to tuck them under the top button on each side in order to keep them in place. It is at least a tenable theory. In no other military photograph of Lee did he find it necessary to place his lapels under restraint.

This is one of only two war-time photographs of General Lee which expose the right side of his face.

THE ONLY WAR-TIME
SKETCH OF LEE

FRANK VIZETELLY, the war correspondent of the *London Illustrated News*, who saw the Southern side of the war largely as a guest of General J. E. B. Stuart and his staff, made this sketch of Lee in the field. It is evidently a random impression, and Lee probably was unaware that it was being made. While it is not particularly revealing and is perhaps not entirely consistent with our idea of Lee, it nevertheless creates an effect of a man of energetic activity. Published in *Harper's Weekly* on March 14, 1863, it has the importance of being the only drawing known to have been made of Lee while the war was in progress.

LEE IN 1863

URNING THE PAGE, the reader will find the first formally posed photograph of the General of the Confederate States' Army of Northern Virginia. It was perhaps in the opening months of 1863, and probably before his illness of late March and early April, that the camera achieved Lee's initial full-length portrait. He was then in his fifty-sixth year, a man nearly six feet in height—erect, well proportioned, robust, of imposing natural dignity. All these things are in the photograph shown on page 39, taken in the studio of the Richmond photographers, Minnis and Cowell. Wearing the invisible laurels of recent victories with grave modesty, he stood for them in the full battle dress of a Confederate general. It is an impressive photograph, well posed and well lighted. He is wearing his field sword, an accoutrement to be seen in only one other photograph. One detail is unique to this portrait: he holds in his right hand a black felt hat with a narrow strip of gold around it. He is gloved and booted for the field, and is carrying his field glasses. The coat is that of a plain Brigadier, with the Confederacy's three-star insignia of a full General.

Facing the photograph is the version of it that was seen in the Northern press. This fine photograph in some way came into the hands of *Harper's Weekly,* appearing as an engraving in the issue of Saturday, July 2, 1864. It serves to show how much of the spirit of a photograph could be lost in a nineteenth-century engraving. Only the superficial aspect is here: the brow, eyes, and nose do not have the noble distinction of the original. One year after Gettysburg, the millions of readers who depended on the Northern press for their information still did not know what their great adversary really looked like. Nor in fact did millions of Southerners know the features of their defender.

General Lee's son, Robert Edward, included this photograph in his book of memoirs of his father, dating it "1862 or 1863." Early 1863 is the more likely date, however, as *Harper's* stated that "the photograph from which our engraving is made bears the stamp of its legal registration in 1863, in the district court of the Confederate states for the Eastern district of Virginia."

The *Harper's Weekly* Engraving.

The Minnis and Cowell Photograph.

THE VANNERSON "BLOCKADE" PORTRAITS

EARLY IN 1864, General Lee yielded to the ladies. Putting aside his dislike of sitting for photographs, he went to the studio of J. Vannerson on the corner of Fourteenth and Main Streets, Richmond. He had placed himself in the hands of a capable craftsman whose work ranked with the best Brady had to offer and who had made many photographs of Richmond notables and soldiers. He was doing this at the entreaty of several Richmond women who wanted new pictures of him. A worthy project was involved—a young Virginia sculptor, Edward V. Valentine, then studying in Berlin, was to make a small statue of General Lee, for sale at a Confederate Bazaar that was to be held in Liverpool for the benefit of disabled Confederate veterans. The relations of the Confederacy with Britain might benefit too—there was still hope of recognition—, and Lee lent himself to the undertaking in a mood of finest compliance, though after what urging from Mrs. Lee we do not know. At all events, he put himself in fullest dress, with every evidence of care as to his appearance. And in the three portraits which follow we are aware of a courtly formality that shows his determination not to fall below the spirit of the occasion.

Vannerson is supposed to have taken four views. Only three are extant. Normally, a sculptor would need at least six views to enable him to build a reconstruction from photographs: right profile, left profile, three-quarters right, three-quarters left, full face, and standing. Possibly Vannerson tried them all, but may not have succeeded in every one. What we have is the left profile, the standing view, and the three-quarters view from the left. The standing view is especially notable in that General Lee is wearing both his military sash and his dress sword—the only time he was ever photographed in his sash.

Next day Mrs. Lee wrote a letter to the sister of the sculptor, Mrs. Wm. F. Gray (Elizabeth Ann Valentine), who apparently had been active on the committee of ladies. It is to be regretted that she did not date her letter:

My dear Madam:

Gen. Lee went to Vannerson's yesterday and had the photographs taken for you. I do not know if they are completed but you can see them or whether they will answer your purpose. I should like to see them before you send them away.

Yrs. truly
M. C. Lee

(Incidentally, Mary Custis Lee never allowed any new likeness of the General, whether photograph or painting, to pass without her "official" sanction.)

The photographs were sent to Valentine in Berlin through the Union blockade. His diary notes that he received them on May 5, 1864. A letter from him mentioned also "the other original portrait." We can only speculate as to which one this was; it was presumably one of the military photographs already reproduced in this book. On May 19th his diary recorded his "putting the clay on the irons for the statuette of General Lee." But he did not complete the work in time for the Liverpool bazaar. On November 9, 1864, Valentine's diary reveals that it was at last finished, photographed, and sent by express to London, to be exhibited in the window of a promi-

nent shop in the West End. Its final destination, the sculptor said, was Scotland. Whether the statue still exists is not known, but photographs made of it in Europe are extant, and a description has also survived. On February 2nd, 1865, the *London Index*, the organ in England of the Confederate Government, printed the following account of it by the editor, John R. Thompson:

"The statuette represents the noble leader of our armies as he might be supposed to stand overlooking the field of battle, the right hand holding his field-glass, the left resting on the hilt of his sword, which the commanding general rarely has occasion to unsheath. The attitude is really majestic, and has been greatly admired. Anything so noble and yet so true to nature is very rarely seen in the works of sculptors whose fame is well established."

Two views of the Valentine statuette, twenty inches high, as photographed in Europe. The Vannerson photographs apparently had not given the young sculptor an adequate idea of Lee's stature.

When he dressed himself for the ordeal of the Vannerson photographs, Lee apparently made a gallant gesture of deference to the committee of Richmond ladies. In later years, when an effort was made to assemble and catalogue the likenesses of Robert E. Lee, Custis Lee said that his father had put on, for the occasion, one of some high shirt-collars presented to him by the ladies. Though the son had apparently confused a later portrait photograph with this series, the reference to a "full length picture" makes it seem that he must have had in mind the Vannerson group.

The Vannerson portraits were widely circulated. They soon took form as lithographs and engravings, eventually appearing in London newspapers and periodicals. Over the years, the fine portrait shown on page 49 has perhaps been the dominant influence on the scores of artists who have sought to recreate Robert E. Lee, but the profile view on page 41 has made an impression almost as deep.

At left is a daguerreotype which is believed never to have been published before. In 1865 General Lee gave it to Dr. George Hatley Norton, a clergyman, of Alexandria, Virginia. It was made from a print from the original Vannerson negative of the portrait photograph shown opposite. Though the process reversed the face, the daguerreotype deserves study for its own special quality of revealing detail.

The Vannerson photograph was engraved on steel by W. E. Marshall. This is a cold and not very successful likeness. In the process, much of the detail of eyes and skin was lost. The mouth took on a definition not like that of the subject, and in general a certain warmth that the camera succeeded in capturing even through Lee's reserve has not been held.

In the early summer of 1869, Lee signed his name to the preface he had written for a new edition of his father's book on the American Revolution, *Memoirs of the War in the Southern Department of the United States*, and sent it to the publisher in New York. The latter wanted to include a portrait of R. E. Lee himself. Lee was reluctant, but after much urging he selected—or perhaps the choice was Mrs. Lee's—the Vannerson portrait. The publisher had O'Neill, the talented engraver, make from it the steel engraving shown above, and when the new edition of Henry Lee's work appeared in the last year of Lee's life, this engraving was in it.

Later the somewhat more finished engraving shown above was to be seen in art reviews and magazines of the nineties. Though a good likeness, it makes a subtle departure from the effect of the original by giving head and shoulders a slightly less erect posture. Lee had been dead for a quarter of a century before Americans saw an adequate rendering of his finest military photograph. It is reproduced on the facing page.

Best of all, and a really admirable example, is this engraving on wood by G. Kruell, executed in 1898. It is one of the finest engravings ever made of Lee. The whole photograph has been rendered faithfully, even to the highlights and hair style.

LEE IN 1864

SOMEWHAT LATER IN 1864, another Richmond photographer, J. W. Davies, made this picture. What is shown opposite is an enlargement of a photograph in *carte* size, with masked background. Though this portrait seems not to have existed in a larger original negative, it was a favorite with the General and with Mrs. Lee; they gave away many autographed copies to solicitous admirers.

In this picture Lee had begun to trim his beard shorter than had been his wont earlier in the war, as comparison with preceding photographs in this book will show. It will be recalled that Lee had worn a full beard for only three years. The fact that he seems to have come gradually to the habit of wearing it in closer style is a detail that helps somewhat to establish the probable sequence of undated photographs. Throughout the rest of his life his beard will be seen much as it appears here.

It was apparently to an extensively retouched copy of this photograph that his son, G. W. C. Lee, attached the note reproduced on an earlier page, pointing out that a group of pictures, of which this was assumed to be one, could be identified by the high shirt-collar which some Richmond ladies had made for General Lee, and which he wore out of compliment to them when he sat for his picture. Circumstances explained on page 44 indicate that the Vannerson group of portraits was the one in question. If the present photograph really shows one of the high gift collars, the General's compliment to the ladies grows higher with it, for this collar seems not to have fitted him very well.

This steel engraving by O'Neill appeared in 1866 to illustrate an anonymous book entitled: *Southern Generals, Who They Are and What They Have Done.* Though it offers a fair likeness, it is by no means an ideal copy of the facing photograph.

At left, a print of the *carte* photograph with the background retouched in the popular vignette style. The autograph is apparently not General Lee's. This photograph was the model for the United States commemorative stamp issue of the United States Army in 1937.

From General Lee's own hand to little Virginia Morgan came this rare original print of the vignetted photograph, reproduced below in a slight reduction with a crack in the venerable and treasured print clearly showing. Beside the photograph is a facsimile of the inscription later written on the back when Virginia Morgan was Mrs. J. Enders Robinson. Presumably she was a guest in the Lee home when she received it. The autograph is Lee's own.

Since this photograph was a favorite with Mrs. Lee, we can ascribe to her wifely vigilance the fact that the General's slightly disordered tie had been retouched in the negative to establish a semblance of neatness by eliminating the dangling end.

Given to me by Gen. Robert E. Lee when I was a child. I was at his home very often.

Signed
Virginia Morgan Robin
(Mrs. J. Enders Robinson)
113 S. 3rd St.
Richmond
Virginia

Just how admirably the nineteenth-century engraver on steel could catch the spirit of a photograph is illustrated by this rendition dating from the 1880's. The engraver was A. B. Hall. Readers who saw this reproduction saw Lee.

THE AUTUMN OF THE CONFEDERACY

IN PETERSBURG, later in 1864, Lee was photographed for the first time on his fine gray horse Traveller. As usual, this picture cannot be dated precisely. Under Traveller's hooves, however, and on the walk, is something that is undoubtedly rubble from shelling (there are broken panes in the building in the background). An examination of the print under an enlarging glass indicates, however, that the rubble is mixed with fallen leaves. Probably autumn was already well advanced; this photograph may have been taken in the last days of October or sometime in November.

Lee was then under a heavy burden. Though there is no hint of discouragement in the set of these shoulders, the twilight that presaged eventual defeat had begun to settle down upon the Confederacy. The war was going badly. Early had met with disaster in the Valley. The thinly held Richmond-Petersburg line had been defended against Federal attempts to outflank it, but as yet there was no assurance that operations would not be resumed before winter. With November, raw, wet weather came on. Lee's men were underfed, dirty, and cold, for food and fuel were insufficient and there was no soap. Desertion was growing alarmingly. In Virginia, Federal operations had come practically to a standstill, but farther south there were ominous developments. In the middle of November Sherman began his march across Georgia to the sea, and when this picture was taken Lee already may have been facing the certainty that Georgia and the Gulf States were to be cut off from Virginia.

As the year went out, bad news piled up: Hood's army had been smashed; Sherman, now at Savannah, was free to start north up the coast; Grant's force was growing overwhelmingly. Through it all, Lee, though he was looking older, let men see no outward sign of despair; the anxiety he must have felt showed itself only in constant activity. The impression here is of a moment's impatient halt in a brisk tour of inspection.

Traveller, in this his first appearance before the camera, was seven years old. His master always gave close attention to his horse's comfort, to his shoeing and girthing; he dismounted often to rest him. When astride in the field Lee usually carried for armament only a pistol in his left holster.

APPOMATTOX

ODERN NEWS PHOTOGRAPHY was in its beginnings in the War Between the States, and like many another tyro it missed its greatest opportunity. No photographer, Confederate or Union, saw the surrender at Appomattox Court House. Mathew Brady was eighty miles away as the crow flies, taking pictures in the vacated Confederate fortifications in front of Petersburg; due to inadequate communications he had not heard of the imminence of surrender. If he had been put specially on the alert, he might have been on hand to photograph arrivals and departures, but it is unlikely that he would have been allowed to enter the room of the McLean house where a man sat waiting, the man who had said: "There is nothing left me but to go and see General Grant, and I would rather die a thousand deaths."

During the half hour before Grant arrived—Dr. Douglas Freeman, Lee's biographer, has called it "perhaps the longest half hour in Lee's whole life"—he was almost alone and certainly little observed. Col. Orville E. Babcock, Grant's aide, was there, and Col. Charles Marshall, who was Lee's nephew and aide; no doubt Wilmer McLean, still surprised at suddenly finding himself host to such a meeting, was in and out of the room making nervous preparations.

Though there has been a supposition that an apparently hasty rough sketch in pen and pencil set down by the great Thomas Nast was his own hurried impression as he looked in the door at Lee, there is no historical foundation for such an idea. Cyril Nast, a son, is authority for the statement that Thomas Nast was not at Appomattox.

Almost thirty years after the surrender, when Nast was near the end of his active career, H. H. Kohlsaat commissioned him to do a large historical painting of the scene. That painting, entitled "Peace in Union," was completed and now hangs in the Museum of Galena, Illinois, which was Grant's home town and Kohlsaat's birthplace. A photograph of it is shown on page 123 of this book. Several years later, Nast undertook another painting, showing Lee in his agony of waiting. This second painting, still unfinished when Nast died in 1902, was apparently based on a rough sketch. Both the sketch and the uncompleted picture are shown here.

Nast's rough sketch may be accounted for in two ways. Soon after the war's end he perhaps encountered or sought out one of the eye-witnesses and set down on paper what the latter remembered having seen. But there is a strong probability that the sketch was made three decades later, when Nast was at work on the Kohlsaat commission, and that it was, in a sense, a by-product of his research for that painting.

In 1895, when Thomas Nast was at work on "Peace in Union," he was living in Morristown, New Jersey. A number of the Federal officers who had followed Grant into the McLean house came out to the Nast home to see the painting in progress. Of the two men who waited with Lee before Grant's arrival, Colonel Babcock had died in 1884; he never wrote of Appomattox and left no record of what he saw there. But Colonel Marshall, still of active mind, was Nast's most helpful Confederate visitor at Morristown.

Cyril Nast, who was then a youth of sixteen, says that Marshall was deeply impressed by the painting being executed for Kohlsaat. It seemed to fill him with excitement, and he showed the warmest interest in working out with Nast the correct detail of the scene. He stayed for several hours, so long that he almost missed his train back to Baltimore. Although the son does not recall seeing it done, he thinks that on that afternoon Nast and Marshall worked out together the idea for another painting of Lee. Looking at this sketch, one feels that Nast made it with someone looking over his shoulder, offering corrections. Note that Nast roughed in the sword in three different positions, altered the placing of Marshall's figure behind Lee, set down in the corner a small croquis showing detail of hands and gloves and sword—the effect is exactly as if he had been trying, as the sketch proceeded, to evoke from the other man's memory the fading details of something that had happened thirty years before.

The words scrawled by Nast on the margin of the rough sketch are contained in Lee's letter to Grant of April 8th, the day before the surrender took place.

Thomas Nast's rough sketch is eloquent. On the premise that it derives directly from Colonel Marshall as an eye-witness, it is included here as the only near approach to a true visual image of Lee at Appomattox. In the unfinished painting, Babcock stands at the window watching for Grant; Marshall is dimly seen behind Lee. The physical details of room and furnishings are exact.

If Nast had lived to finish the painting, one of the alterations he had in mind, according to Cyril Nast, was to introduce traces of black in hair and beard; he felt that he had made them too white. That the change was needed is shown by the group of Brady photographs that immediately follows.

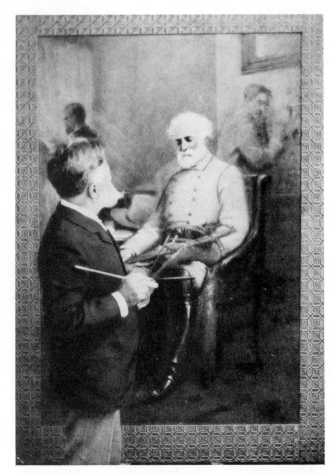

Thomas Nast at work on the painting.

THE MAN WHO CAME HOME

THE PHOTOGRAPHERS again caught up with General Lee not long after his return to Richmond on April 15. When news of the surrender reached Mathew Brady in Petersburg, he and his assistant gathered together their equipment and drove a hundred miles to the McLean house. In the room of the signing they found nothing to photograph but emptiness. Souvenir hunters had bought or appropriated all movable articles. They had cleaned out everything—tables, lamp, chairs, pictures, pen, inkstand. Brady hurried to Richmond over the same route Lee had taken; he was going with the sole purpose of making portraits of the General. There seemed to be a fair prospect of getting what he wanted—for, after all, had he not known Lee for many years? "It was supposed," he told one of the war correspondents, "that it would be preposterous to ask him to sit, but I thought that would be the time for the historical picture."

General Lee, however, was immured in his home in Franklin Street. Wanting only isolation and rest, he spent much of the time in bed or sitting quietly in a chair in the back parlor. But he could not remain undisturbed for long. Soon the whole world seemed to be at his door—old officers, ministers and public men, devoted soldiers, women whose loved ones were missing, journalists, Federal officers. His family spared him all they could, and among others whom they politely turned away was Brady. But Brady did not give up after the first refusal. "Of course, I had known him since the Mexican War when he was on General Scott's staff," he said, "and my request was not as from an intruder." So he went to an intimate friend, General Robert Ould, Federal commissioner of prisoners, and Ould prevailed on Mrs. Lee to prevail in turn on the General.

On the following day Brady was permitted to come to the house and was allowed one hour to photograph Lee on the lower back porch. He thought that would give him time enough to make five plates. (He actually made six, but of these only four of the glass negatives now exist, though there is an imperfect print from another.) When the photographer had his camera set up and the plates coated, a chair was brought out and General Lee emerged, dressed in the new uniform he had worn for his meeting with General Grant.

Brady took six pictures. The five which survive comprise two of Lee seated and flanked by one of his sons, presumably General W. H. F. Lee, and by Colonel Walter Taylor; one of Lee alone, seated with his left profile presented to the camera; and two standing poses. One of the latter, though it must have been a revealing picture, exists only in a hazy copy; the other is an outstanding portrait judged by any standard. There was little conversation, Brady said later, though Lee changed his position readily under the photographer's direction; he was still the soldier going through with what he must do.

But the camera has caught his true feelings. The tense strain of war is still upon him, and he is here facing up to another ordeal. His bearing is closely controlled, his gaze in two views is sharply direct; but in all the pictures his eyes are shadowed with suffering, his jaw is set. It is a remarkable group of photographs.

The Man Who Came Home from Appomattox

General Lee photographed by Brady in Richmond. One of his sons, probably "Rooney," stands at his right, Colonel Walter Taylor at his left.

The same group photographed from another angle. Clearly seen here is the cross formed by the panelling of the door. The Virginia Historical Society points out that this design was widely used in doorway architecture throughout the South, as a symbol of the protection of the Christian spirit over those who lived within.

This photograph exists only in an old copy, the original negative having been lost. The print from which the copy was made had been masked to make it an oval, and in processing some of the sharpness was lost. There is evidence that Lee may have liked this view himself. Soon after Brady took the pictures, young Captain J. O. Armes, who had served on Gen. W. S. Hancock's staff at Cold Harbor, was visiting his brother in Richmond. On the street he encountered his boyhood friend, Dan Lee, a nephew of Robert E. Lee. In his memoirs Armes relates that young Lee greeted him warmly and invited him to his uncle's house. Leaving after an hour or two, the young Union captain was presented with a print of this photograph. General Lee autographed it, and, said Armes, "I shall never forget the sad expression of his face as the General shook hands and bade me goodbye."

It is illuminating to compare this profile view taken by Brady with the similar view on page 41, taken by Vannerson not much more than a year earlier, when the Southern cause, though declining, was still one of hope.

When a travelling photographer from Lynchburg visited the Lee home in Lexington several years later he was startled to see that Mrs. Lee was using a special enlargement of this photograph as a fire screen; to his surprised query she replied laughing that it was "the best use" she could make of it, and moreover "it fitted very snugly in that place."

PICTURE PUZZLE

ABOVE, AT RIGHT, is a portrait of Lee now in the collection of the Virginia Historical Society. It is the work of Edward Caledon Bruce, who was born in Winchester, Virginia, in 1825 and died in 1901. His career in portraiture was achieved against the handicap of total deafness from the age of thirteen, due to an attack of scarlet fever.

The Virginia Historical Society believes this to have been painted from life, a study or sketch for a larger canvas which has been lost to view. In 1896 Bruce himself described this larger canvas in a letter now in the files of the Valentine Museum, Richmond. The painter wrote in part:

"My best known picture is perhaps the full length life-size of Lee, painted in Richmond and begun at Petersburg from life, in the fall of the winter of '64-'65. It was exhibited in the State Capitol in Feb'y. '65, where numbers of Confederate officers and soldiers saw it, and I was told that their judgment was highly favorable. It represents the General standing by a captured gun, red lined cloak resting on the wheel and his grey horse in background held by his courier. The details are all from reality."

Bruce goes on to say that the canvas was exhibited in various places in the East after the war, and as far north as Montreal. Then it was put in storage, to emerge twenty years later considerably damaged because it had been rolled up the wrong way. It was much in need of repair by the artist *"except in the face and surrounding parts."* In 1896, when the letter was written, the painting was the property of Charles Broadway Rouss of New York City, and was always prominently displayed at the reunions of the Southern Society of New York. "*The head and figure still stand well,*" wrote Bruce, "the former coming out of the canvas with great effect."

C. B. Rouss, the owner of the canvas, died in 1902. Today the whereabouts of the painting is not known.

By the Virginia Historical Society's theory, this would be the study made in Petersburg from life in the war's last winter, and later transferred by Bruce to his larger canvas. Although it seems unlike Lee, especially when compared with the contemporary photographs, it must be borne in mind that Lee's appearance varied greatly from time to time with the degree to which his hair and beard were trimmed.

At left on the facing page is a canvas now in the possession of the Pennsylvania Academy of the Fine Arts. It is signed "C W B 1865," and has been ascribed to C. W. Bruckner, of whose work as a portraitist there is practically no record. All that is known is that the painting was sold at auction in New York City in 1920. The Academy's efforts to trace it to its origin have been unsuccessful.

Obviously the two portraits shown side by side are related. An examination of the one at the left has disclosed that it had been "relined". The area containing the head is an oval-shaped piece, cut out from another canvas and mounted on a rectangle. In spite of the work of the restorer, who added indifferently painted uniformed shoulders and body to the canvas surrounding the mounted piece, the photograph has innocently picked up the line of the oval. At once the theory rises to mind that this had been done to make a portrait feature of the "*face and surrounding parts*" which had been little damaged in the period of storage. This, then, may be the central part of the large painting by Edward Caledon Bruce, with the heroic background cut away; it has been reworked into a semblance of conventional portraiture. The signature "C W B 1865" would have been added by another hand, and may well have been a misreading of a badly damaged original signature which had read "E C B 1865."

Both these portraits can make a strong claim to authenticity as life portraiture. The one at right is undoubtedly the quick study made from life in the last winter of the war; the portrait at left is quite possibly the central fact in the canvas which the painter derived from that study.

"HE IS GETTING OLD, LIKE HIS MASTER"

IT WAS THE MIDDLE OF SEPTEMBER, 1865, when the General, on Traveller, set out from "Derwent," the tenant-farmer cottage in Powhatan County which had been the Lees' home during the summer. Three days later man and horse wound up their 108-mile journey in Lexington, and Lee took up his duties as the new president of Washington College. His family was to follow as soon as was practicable. On the long ride Lee wore a uniform of gray from which he had removed all insignia and Confederate buttons; probably he was wearing the identical habit when the accompanying photograph was taken, just one year later.

In midsummer of 1866, Alexander Gardner, Brady's former studio manager and assistant, had made a joint effort with Miley, the Lexington photographer, to get a picture of Lee on Traveller. There was insistent demand for such a picture. But it was hot, the flies were annoying, and Traveller's restiveness spoiled all attempts. In September Miley tried again, with the result shown on the following page. This photograph become one of the most popular of Lee's pictures all through the South, and was widely adapted and elaborated.

Traveller shared his master's fame, but shared also the penalties, for so much of his mane and tail was tweaked out by souvenir hunters that the horse grew nervous in the presence of strangers. He outlived Lee, dying finally of tetanus.

In the years after the war, Lee found great comfort in him. He truly loved the horse that had carried him through most of the fighting, and to him he gave an affectionate care touching to see. To Martha ("Markie") Williams, who intended making a portrait of Traveller, Lee wrote this description:

"If I were an artist like you, I would draw a true picture of Traveller; representing his fine proportions, muscular figure, deep chest, short back, strong haunches, flat legs, small head, broad forehead, delicate ears, quick eye, small feet and black mane and tail. Such a picture would inspire a poet, whose genius could then depict his worth and describe his endurance of toil, hunger, thirst, heat and cold, and the dangers and sufferings through which he passed. He could dilate upon his sagacity and affection, and his invariable response to every wish of his rider. He might even imagine his thoughts through the long night-marches and days of battle through which he has passed. But I am no artist Markie, and can therefore only say he is a Confederate grey."

"Markie" had wanted a photograph of Traveller. Lee sent one—we can only speculate which of those shown in this book it was—and in January of 1868 he sent a letter to the artist asking about progress on Traveller's portrait. "He is getting old, like his master," Lee wrote, "and looks to your portrait to hand him down to posterity."

The Miley Photograph of Lee on Traveller.

An original lithograph executed by A. Hoen and Company of Richmond from the Miley photograph. Copyrighted in 1876, it was generally circulated. The lithograph is fairly faithful to the photograph of man and mount and does not widely depart from the actual background, though there has been some embellishment, and details have been sharpened throughout.

Widely known was this oil painting by David Bendann. Miley's photograph was clearly the model, but the painter took many liberties. The changes he made in Lee and in the stance of the horse, his romanticizing of the background, have not enhanced the subject.

AT THE ROCKBRIDGE BATHS

THERE WAS ONE TIME when Lee showed himself open to approach by a photographer; perhaps it was because the man was a Confederate veteran. It is to be deplored that the results that have come down to us are not very revealing. The Lee family spent the summer of 1866 at the Rockbridge Baths, some ten miles from Lexington, and it was there that A. H. Plecker of Lynchburg came up to Lee. After four years of fighting he had resumed his old profession, equipped himself with what he called a "car,"—he styled it "A. H. Plecker's Travelling Gallery"—and commenced travelling the countryside taking pictures.

"Yes, I will," promptly said the General, when Plecker asked for a sitting. "But how would you like to take me? On my horse?"

"Any way you like," said the surprised man, and the appointment was arranged.

A few days later General Lee reported to the photographer, mounted. Again mid-summer heat and flies unsettled the redoubtable Traveller and he spoiled several plates, but Plecker finally got two which he considered satisfactory. Then, apparently, he made others of Lee; he recorded that Lee "came into the car and made some small bust photos, one of which Mrs. Lee said was the best picture of him to that time." This was no light compliment, for Mrs. Lee was critical, and it is unfortunate that these photographs have not survived. Two photographs of Lee mounted on Traveller have been preserved, but the one not shown is one of those that Traveller's restiveness spoiled; moreover the whole surface is too badly reticulated for reproduction. When Plecker returned to Lynchburg, he enlarged both the photographs included here to impressive dimensions, elaborating the mounted pose in water colors and the other in oils. Of the latter a photograph of this colored version survives, but no print from the original negative. Plecker distributed postcard prints of the upper photograph widely.

Traveller's uneasiness obliged the photographer to focus his camera on the horse rather than the rider.

A photograph of the colored rendering which Plecker made of the original.

THE RETURN TO WASHINGTON

THE PHOTOGRAPHS OF TRAVELLER and his master have shown nothing of what time was doing to the man who from 1861 to 1865 had carried a burden that must have been almost beyond the bearing. Indeed, after the revealing photographs taken by Brady on the back porch in Richmond, there is a gap of perhaps four years in examples of true portrait photographs. The dates of many of the late pictures are uncertain, but this date is clear: in early May of 1869 the face of Robert E. Lee again came before the camera. Again the work was Brady's, and once more the eye of the camera was searching.

In the latter part of April, 1869, Lee had gone to Baltimore, under heavy pressure from his friends and associates, to lend his influence to what he considered a worthy undertaking—a project for securing capital to establish a railroad that would serve the Shenandoah Valley. On May 1st he proceeded to Washington to pay his respects to President Grant, in response to an invitation from the White House. The brief and somewhat formal interview, lasting perhaps fifteen minutes, apparently had no political significance so far as the South was concerned, and no satisfactory account of it was recorded. On May 3rd or 4th the General went on by steamer to Alexandria. But he had spent several days in Washington, and had found occasion to go to the gallery of Mathew Brady. Lee's presence in Washington had not gone unnoticed, and probably Brady had pleaded for a sitting—his insistence had succeeded with Lee before. History cannot regret his importunings. This was the last time he was to see Lee.

The three very fine portraits which follow were the result. They show with startling effect what the war had done to General Lee. When his family were finally established in Lexington in the autumn of 1865 he had seemed bright and even gay, but the next several years were to show that the long strain had taken its toll. His illness in the spring before Chancellorsville, the illness which probably followed soon after the taking of the picture shown on page 39, had been the start of a physical deterioration. In the after-war years, Lee knew much pain. What he regarded as rheumatism was probably angina pectoris; hardening of the arteries was rapid after 1866, and he had some arthritis. From his symptoms these conditions seem to us now to have been clearly evident in the last two years of his life, and when Brady took these pictures, Lee had only eighteen months to live.

May, 1869, in Washington. This is one of three notable views, taken over a space of five years, that bring the left profile into sharp definition. The two earlier ones are to be found on pages 41 and 65.

Another of the Brady poses, perhaps the most eloquent of all. Camera portraiture may have taken on new subtleties, but it has never surpassed this in simple honesty.

The third Brady photograph shows Lee in the famous Brady chair beside the Brady clock, recognizable from so many of the notable camera studies of the era. In the author's opinion, this is the finest portrait of General Lee, and Brady's best effort.

Again the gap between the distinguished reality and the inadequate version that the great news-reading public saw. This engraving with its improvised background was made by Robin and appeared in *Harper's Weekly* in 1869. The change in posture, the sharpening of values in eyes and mouth, bring with them a loss of something hard to define: an essential fineness, a sympathetic quality long since familiar to the reader of these pages.

From this point on, it again becomes difficult to assign dates to the photographs. It does not matter greatly—the rest were all made in the very last years of Lee's life. When Custis Lee catalogued the Lee pictures some years after his father's death, of most of these he could only say, "between 1865 and 1870." Some of the examples he supplied were highly retouched; some of them were even photographs of lithographs derived from photographs.

Sometimes details of dress serve to reveal that two apparently unrelated photographs were made at the same sitting. The fine and very late photograph shown above was made by Boude and Miley of Lexington. To the same photographers must be ascribed the original of the small *carte* photograph reproduced at right, even though the *carte* was trademarked by Fraser and Rees of Richmond. The bow tie, which is unlike the bow tie in any other photograph, the waistcoat with rounded lapels—these are clearly the same, and they appear in combination only in these two photographs.

AT THE WHITE SULPHUR SPRINGS

B Y THE TIME LEE made his next-to-last visit to the White Sulphur, in the then new
state of West Virginia, Traveller's trot had become definitely too hard for him on a long
trip, though it had been Traveller who had carried him when the Lees first went there
two summers earlier. That visit in 1867 had been made for the benefit of Mrs. Lee's
arthritis, but in the next two seasons doctor's orders sent Lee back for his own good—the waters
might help his "rheumatism," which in reality was probably a serious heart condition.

In this August of 1869 as always, Lee sought to avoid the society of the older men, for they
seemed obsessed by two subjects he tried to stay clear of: the war and politics. On the occasion,
however, when these two views were taken he must have found himself pitched right into the midst
of the tabooed topics, for the back row is an impressive lineup of Confederates. Left to right are
Brigadier General James Connor, Brigadier General Martin W. Gary, Major General John Bank-
head Magruder, Brigadier General Robert D. Lilley, General P. G. T. Beauregard, Brigadier

General A. R. Lawton, Brigadier General Henry A. Wise, and Brigadier General Joseph L. Brent. Seated at Lee's right is Blacque Bey, Turkish envoy, while to his left are George Peabody, W. W. Corcoran, philanthropists, and James Lyons, a lawyer of Richmond.

All these men except the Turkish envoy remained remarkably immobile while the two plates were made. But not Lee. He dropped his hat; he shifted in his chair in a way that suggests discomfort, even pain. And by that time pain was almost always with him. A new impression of bodily frailty here reaches the camera; there is no longer an effect of physical composure that cannot be shaken.

R E Lee

Boude and Miley made this photograph, which has no precise date. It took on an influence as enduring as any other photograph of Lee in his last years. In the second section of this book, the section entitled "From the Legend," the reader will observe that many of the posthumous portraits of Lee, artists' reconstructions of him in this final phase of his life, were inspired mainly by this photograph. Judge J. Fisher of Sutton, W. Va., who was a student at Washington and Lee University in Custis Lee's presidency, has evidence that convinces him that this was Lee's last picture.

This view deserves special study, for it is one of the only two photographs of Robert E. Lee which show him in sharply defined right profile. Mr. D. W. Thomas, president of the Chesapeake Western Railway, believes it to have been the last one taken. In a sense, his contention and that in favor of the photograph reproduced opposite support rather than contradict one another, for on the evidence of similarities in dress and photographic finish, both pictures can be assigned to the same sitting.

THE THIRD PORTRAIT

JUST A YEAR before his fatal illness, Lee sat to a painter for his portrait, the third in his lifetime. The first (page 15) had been painted when he was thirty-one; at the time of the second (page 23) he was nearing fifty. He was now sixty-two. The artist was Frank Buchser, a Swiss portraitist of considerable reputation. Almost fiercely independent in forming his opinions, he was a man of warm sympathies and strong dislikes. Buchser spent the years from 1866 to 1871 in the United States. In those five years he achieved many portraits of outstanding Americans, among them William Cullen Bryant, General W. T. Sherman, and William H. Seward. For the latter, as for most of the political figures of Washington, he conceived an outright contempt, violently phrased in his journal.

Buchser arrived in Lexington on the 25th of September, 1869, having come expressly to paint Lee. Three weeks of work lay ahead; on days when Lee could not sit, the artist made drawings in the town or in the countryside. On the evening of the eighteenth of October a reception was held at Lee's home, presumably to honor the painter and the completed portrait. With a few quick strokes Buchser sketched the gathering. On the twenty-second of October he left by the canal-boat *Percy*, bearing away the completed portrait.

Before the sittings could begin, it had been necessary to settle an important question: How was Lee to be painted? His intimates wanted him in Confederate uniform, but Lee supported Buchser's preference for a simple frock coat. "I am a soldier no longer," he said, "and it is time to put aside the pomp and circumstance of war." As a concession to military atmosphere, however, on a table beside him were placed his uniform, his dress sword and sword-belt, his sash, hat, and field glasses.

Fortunately Buchser was a diarist and letter-writer, and in 1942 these personal records were published posthumously in Switzerland.* His Swiss editor and annotator believes that his conversations with Lee may well have been more extensive than the entries in his diary indicate; he points out that Buchser was intent on setting down any details that seemed important to a projected picture of Lee's surrender to Grant at Appomattox Court House. Apparently he never painted that picture.

The first record of the sitting is translated from the German of Buchser's diary.

3 October 1869, Lexington Va.

. . . General Robert E. Lee is sitting to me for his portrait, and if I paint him and Grant together, for example the surrender at Appomattox Court House, we shall have the ultimate illustration, the great finale of the strife that seemed from a distance to be a war on a titanic scale.

Only yesterday Lee said to me that in no battle did he ever have more than 50,000 men at his disposition. If that's the way it was, let's have as little noise as possible about the whole matter. What a fine, noble soul, good and lovable, the old white-haired warrior is! I am coming to the conviction that if the American statesmen of the last fifteen years had been half as astute and only half as honorable and able as the soldiers, such as Generals Grant, Lee, Sherman, etc., the war would never have been begun, and once it had been begun, a winter campaign of 500,000 men most certainly would have made an end of the business; three months with Seward have opened my eyes! Grant, Lee, Sherman, all are worth more

---

*Frank Buchser; Mein Leben und Streben in Amerika: Begegnungen und Bekenntnisse eines Schweizer Malers. 1866-1871; eingeleitet und herausgegeben von Gottfried Wälchli; Orell Füssli Verlag, Zürich-Leipzig; 1942.

than the intriguing sneaks and profane frauds of wire-pullers who are called "politicians" in this country! If a great storm should arise and annihilate them in a single blow, one would be able clearly to perceive in it the hand of God, and this land could again be the happiest in the world, as it was before the war.

*　　*　　*　　*

Tomorrow will bring the completion of Lee's head.

Next comes an extract from a letter, dated October 5, 1869, which Buchser wrote to someone in Charlottesville. He wrote in English, with occasional mistakes in idiom and an occasional misspelling, and he underscored several words.

Buchser's sketch of the evening party at the Lee house. At left, the General. At right a feminine group surrounds Mrs. Lee in her invalid chair.

October 5th [18]69
St. . . . Charlottesville.

I had a long conversation with general Lee (to-day during the sitting) of his surrender to Grant. The subject seemed to be painful to him, but as he went on, it wore off. His plan was to go into the Carolinas and continue the war there, but at Appomatox Court House his army had so melted down, that he had scarcely 8000 bayonets left with him. His cavalry opened the lines, broke through the enemy, but it was of no fresh use, and so he wrote to Grant, leaning on former advances of the general of the Union and a meeting was agreed at once. The two generals met between the two armies. They met on horseback*, as much as Lee remembered it, and then went into a house. The meeting was extremely *kind, cordial* and *gentlemanly*. Lee asked Grant what terms he would give if Lee should surrender his army and Grant then made the well-known overtures which Lee thought generous in the extreme. Lee joined in that all or mostly all of the confederate cavalry brought their own horses, to

---

*This incorrect detail is probably due to Buchser's imperfect memory of the conversation. It is unlikely that Lee would have forgotten the half hour he waited for Grant in the McLean house.

which Grant at once said that they might keep their horses etc. Lee then desired Grant to put these terms to paper in the shape of a letter which Grant did so forth. Lee read it carefully over, suggesting a few corrections which Grant agreed to at once. After having done so, Grant gave his letter to his aide, Colonel Parker, or some-one else, which Lee did not exactly remember. The aide copied it, Grant, after reading it over, handed it to Lee, who read it again carefully and expressed himself satisfied, upon which Grant put his signature to it. Upon this, Lee wrote down his surrender of all the arms, ammunition of war, canons and military stores etc., with the exception of the side-arms of the officers, which were granted to them as terms of capitulation honourable. They exchanged the letters, shook hands, as Lee thinks to remember, and they parted. Lee during all this was accompanied by a sole aide, Colonel [Marshall]. Grant had also only one aide with him at the time of the meeting indoor of the farm-house, but by degrees the room began to fill along the wall, out of hearing distance, by officers of Grant's staff. The general Lee was in his full field-uniform "with the very sword and sash you now paint here, Mr. Buchser"; he continued: "I don't like to dwell on this subject, but as it is a matter who now belongs to history, it cannot be helped, and as you intend to paint my surrender, to which I have no objection whatever, I may as well speak to you about it."—

About Jefferson Davis he said that he was, of course, one of the extremest politicians, but otherwise, as a man, one of the purest and noblest that could be found in the world.

Speaking of the war altogether he coincided with me fully that the war was only created by a set of poor politicians, but that it was by no means a necessity and could easily have been avoided, but that the republican party wanted to get control of the country and to obtain this they did not shrink back of anything. If it would have cost still more than it did, it would not have mattered to them, etc.

Of Grant he says that he never liked him so well as at the time of the surrender, that he was then really magnanimous, but since then that he allows himself to be guided almost entirely by the party who elected him, but that he believes that if he (Grant) could follow the dictates of his heart that he would act otherwise. All these things will work around in time. Time, of course, will change everything.

With all this, Lee never uttered one spiteful word against anybody. One cannot see and know this great soldier without loving him.

His portrait progresses well. I painted his left eye today; it is the living eye of this great man. One can read in it the heavy history, the heavy storm his heart underwent.

The following translation is from the diary's final Lexington entry in German:

Thursday, October 7th, 1869

The picture of R. Lee is going to be remarkable. He said to me today that the charge against Wirz* was the most unjust calumny in the world, and consequently his execution was downright judicial murder, in that they, the Confederates, had made every effort to further the exchange of prisoners, a thing which the North never subscribed to. Here Grant personally came in for criticism. Lee asserted that the Confederates finally offered to give their prisoners

---

*Captain Henry Wirz, commander of the interior of Andersonville Military prison, who was tried in August of 1865 on charges of murder, found guilty by a military commission, and hanged.

Detail from the Portrait

freedom without reciprocity if the Union would only supply means of transport. This **too** Grant was said to have refused.

As the Confederates informed the North, they had not enough doctors and medicines for the care of sick prisoners; the United States government whenever possible should provide doctors and medicines for them; these would care for the Union prisoners and not the Confederate troops, if it were so desired; even this was without result. The thing is glaring, **it** positively reeks.

The completed painting went to Europe with the artist and has remained there. Though Buchser was a mannered painter, his portrait of Lee has more of straightforward simplicity, less of contrivance, than his other work in America. Lee's contemporaries, however, were astonished by the air of vigor, the aggressive light in his eyes, the effect almost of burly vitality, an effect which actually is belied by the photographs taken at this period, for example those that have been shown on pages 80 and 81, whose date is late summer, about six weeks earlier.

And yet the portraitist had not been insincere. The explanation of the contradiction is to be found in another book about Buchser recently published in Switzerland,* a book which serves also to illumine the quoted extracts of the artist's conversations with Lee. The Swiss had shown himself an astute psychologist, and when he was ready to transfer an effect to his canvas he had known how to bring back Lee the Warrior.

Day after day the General had appeared and had assumed his pose, in reserved and unbending composure. When the artist had come to the crucial point of getting the facial expression, he began conversationally to explore the subject of Virginia's secession from the Union. There was at first little response; Lee showed his dislike for all talk having to do with the War Between the States.

Buchser persisted; he made it clear that he himself had the greatest interest in certain matters bound up with that period of Virginia's history, and that with him, a foreigner, Lee need not feel the same compulsion to avoid the subject that would rule him in the presence of his own countrymen. Gradually the General relaxed his reserve; soon he was talking freely and in such an intensity of earnestness that his role as model was quite forgotten. Buchser gave him the closest attention, occasionally putting to him a leading question; meanwhile his brush was busy. Old fires had risen and broken through, and the artist succeeded in capturing their glow on his canvas.

The Swiss publication listed below in the footnote includes a color reproduction of a detail of the head as Buchser painted it. Lee's natural coloring was still fairly high in the autumn of 1869. His gray hair and beard still showed definite traces of their original black; under stress of emotion the ruddy tone came flooding back into his face; the brown eyes darkened with the rush of feeling.

On the stand beside Lee are "the very sword and sash you now paint here, Mr. Buchser."

*H. Lüdecke: Frank Buchsers amerikanische Sendung, 1866-1871: die Chronik seiner Reisen; Holbein-Verlag, Basel; 1941.

This Was Lee in the Spring of 1865

For the sake of physical contrast, a pose shown earlier is repeated here. When Lee stood for Brady on the Richmond porch not long after Appomattox he was still the General of the Armies, still the formidable military man in eyes and bearing, with a bodily effect of alertness and vigor. He was fifty-eight, and defeat had not touched his spirit.

This Was Lee Scarcely Four Years Later

Perhaps it was only three years afterwards, (the photograph is assigned to 1868 or 1869), when Lee stood for this picture in the Lexington studio of Boude and Miley. He was at most sixty-two. Almost overnight he had paid the price of the long burden of war. His illness in the spring of 1863 had been one that nowadays would have brought a physician's strict order: Less work, more rest, less strain, less worry. Instead the load had grown; for two years the strain had mounted cruelly, to end at last in the agony of frustration. It had been, after all, too much to bear.

Boude and Miley evidently took this standing pose on the same occasion as the one shown on the preceding page.

THE MEETING IN SAVANNAH

ALL THROUGH THE WINTER of 1869-70, General Lee's health had been especially bad. In almost continual pain, he could walk no farther than to his office, though if he could endure the torture of getting on his horse he could ride Traveller a little in favorable weather. For the most part he could only attend to routine administrative details. Rather than accept his resignation, the faculty of Washington College persuaded him to appoint an acting president and to travel for his health. In this his doctors concurred.

Late in March of 1870 he left Lexington with his daughter Agnes, bound toward a warmer climate, for colds were his great enemy. His journey developed into a long and exhausting tour, full of encounters with former Confederate officers—painful meetings, some of them—, days crowded with receptions and social importunities. Much was warded off, but much could not be. Richmond, next North Carolina, then South Carolina; finally Savannah, with cheering crowds, bands, a demonstration in which even the Federal garrison joined. In the midst of it all, the Savannah *Republican* was aware of a look of "inexpressible sadness" on Lee's face. Then came calls, formalities, a dinner with old comrades—among them General Joseph E. Johnston.

The two had not met since the February before Appomattox. What they said has not been recorded anywhere—one feels that they could have found few words. For the sake of a postwar benevolence, "The Ladies Memorial Association," they were persuaded to go to the Ryan galleries to be photographed, the first and only time they were ever together before the camera. Two plates were made, two photographs of ineffable pathos.

Then on to northern Florida, and return by way of Charleston, Wilmington, Portsmouth and Norfolk, with public demands all the way that even a sick man could not evade. Lee found some rest at the old estates, such as Lower Brandon, Shirley, the White House. Then Richmond again, and home to Lexington after an absence of a little more than two months.

The expanding art of photography had spread his likeness through the South, and people had known in advance how he would look. At way-stations old ladies would put their heads into a car window and say, "He is mighty like his pictures"—so Agnes wrote to her mother.

There had been no real improvement in his health. He himself was sure now that the stricture in his chest was a thing of the heart and was past all curing. "If I attempt to walk beyond a very slow gait, the pain is always there." His biographer, Douglas Freeman, believes that if Lee had not found an interval of quiet at Brandon he would have died before reaching home. In North Carolina he had visited the grave of his daughter Annie, and he felt now that his own end was near.

Robert E. Lee and Joseph E. Johnston at D. Ryan's gallery in Savannah. Each was sixty-three years old. Lee was in his last year of life; Johnston lived to be eighty-four.

By special permission, to aid the Ladies' Memorial Association.

Gen's R. E. LEE and J. E. JOHNSTON

D. J. Ryan, Savannah, Ga.

Entered according to the Act of Congress in the Clerk's Office of the U. S. District Court, Savannah, Ga.

They changed to opposite sides of the table; a photograph less well lighted than the other.

A fine wood engraving of the better of the two photographs reached the great public, appearing in the *Century Magazine* and other publications.

THE VALENTINE SCULPTURES

At right is the portrait bust, at left another clay study of the head.

NOT UNTIL HIS LAST YEAR did Lee sit for direct portrait sculpture. Edward V. Valentine, the young sculptor who had been studying in Berlin and had made a statuette from the Vannerson photographs supplied to him by the ladies, had returned to Virginia after the war. When Lee's exhausting southern tour was nearly over and he had stopped in the capital for a thorough going-over by the Richmond physicians, he went to Valentine's studio in response to urgings. Evidently he liked the young man, for he allowed detailed measurements to be taken for a portrait head. The sculptor said that he would have to do the actual modeling in Lexington. Should he come now or in the fall? Let him come now, said Lee, even though he himself would have more leisure for sittings toward autumn—and Valentine sensed that Lee felt his hold on life to be uncertain.

That was on May 25th, 1870. Lee left for home the next day. Valentine followed eight days later, and finally found for his workroom a vacant store under the hotel. (He had declined Lee's generous offer to clear for him a room in his own house.) The sittings began on June 7th. Fearing the effect on Lee of dampness in a room long unused, Valentine had a fire lighted. Lee sat on a raised stand, uncomplaining, but from time to time unconsciously putting his hand near his heart as if he were in pain. He had asked that the sessions be kept very private: no one was to be admitted except his son Custis and one of the professors.

Lee was kind to a nervous and constrained young man; he even jested to put him at his ease, and soon the two were talking of many things. The making of a faithful portrait in clay is a slow affair, but Lee endured the tedium of the sittings without protest, though he once asked if Custis, who was said to look like him, might not take his place. He even submitted in good nature to another ordeal when the finished head was carried to Mrs. Lee, house-bound by arthritis, for her inspection. Several of Mrs. Lee's friends were present to advise her. For a difficult quarter of an hour, while Valentine turned the bust again and again to show it from all possible angles, Lee turned himself patiently around to afford parallel views. Mrs. Lee's suggestions were doubtless incorporated, and on June 20th the bust was cast.

On the day when Valentine called to pay his parting respects, he heard Lee say to three other callers: "I feel that I have an incurable disease coming on me—old age. I would like to go to some quiet place in the country and rest." It was indeed providential that the sculptor had come in June, for when he said goodbye to Valentine, Lee had less than four months remaining to him.

"If I were asked to name the most characteristic feature of General Lee," Valentine wrote some time afterward, ". . . my answer would be, 'A complete absence of the melodramatic in all that he said and did.' And I may add that an artist, above all other men, is quick to observe the faintest suggestion of posing; the slightest indication of movement or expression which smacks of vanity. . . . Such weaknesses . . . were totally lacking in General Lee."

The eloquent photograph on the facing page has been believed by many to have been Lee's last. A comparison of details of dress with the photograph shown on page 100 suggests that it was taken at the same sitting, which occurred before January 10, 1870. Those shown on pages 82 and 83 may have been the final sitting. All four pictures must be very close in date. The last photographs of Lee to which a date can be assigned were made with Joseph E. Johnston in Savannah, early in April of 1870.

Perhaps the Last Photograph

"Robert Lee was one of the small company of great men in whom there is no inconsistency to be explained, no enigma to be solved. What he seemed, he was—a wholly human gentleman, the essential elements of whose positive character were two and only two, simplicity and spirituality."
—Douglas Southall Freeman in *R. E. Lee*

BOUDE & MILEY,   LEXINGTON, VA.

Lexington Va: 10 Jan't 1870

Miss Jen Campbell
    Jackson La:

            In Compliance
with your request I send you
my Photographs. It is the
last that has been taken & is
the only kind I have. I wish
I had a better
            Very resp't
                R E Lee

Occasionally Lee's correspondence gives us a hint as to the date of a picture. For instance, in January of 1870, nine months before he died, he wrote to a lady in Louisiana that he was sending "the last that has been taken." What he sent was the dim, autographed print shown above at left. It reveals little. A retouched version of this subject came into circulation, however. It modified the signs of age, and is reproduced here to show how deceptive and confused the photographic record can become.

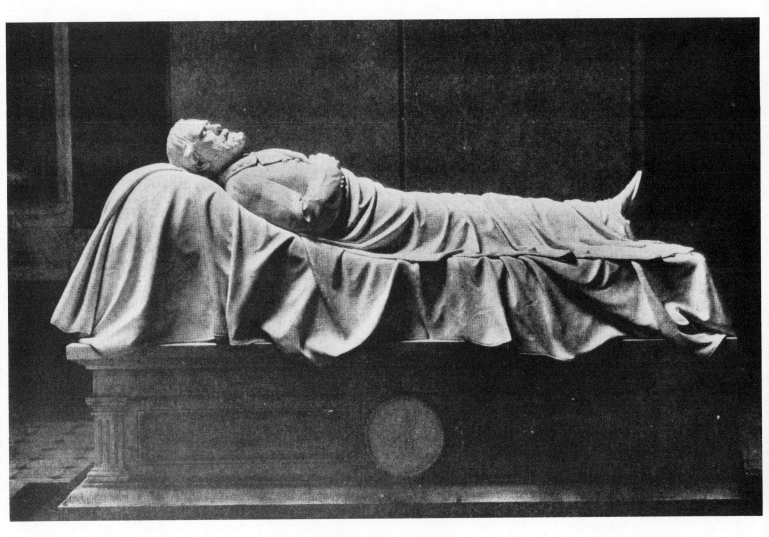

The Recumbent Statue

It rests in the statue chamber of the chapel of Washington and Lee University, Lexington. Executed by Edward V. Valentine on commission, from the measurements and detailed observations he had made in the last year of Lee's life. Lee is entombed with members of his family in the crypt. The detail below is from a plaster cast in the Valentine Museum, Richmond.

The Death Mask
October 12, 1870
The original plaster cast is in the Confederate Museum, Richmond.

FROM THE LEGEND

LIFE ENDED FOR ROBERT E. LEE ON OCTOBER 12, 1870, but his spirit grew on in the affections of a people. Likenesses of him multiplied, likenesses conceived in a fervor of adoration or in a veneration sometimes touched with mysticism. Artists studied Lee's photographs and his portraits, pored over biography and history to gain new flashes of insight, and then tried zealously to recreate on canvas the spirit of his greatness. Engravers on steel and wood still strove to give the public nearer facsimiles of his photographs. Sculptors kept on working at his image. Lithographers and painters of historical subjects applied themselves to showing him meeting great crises, on occasions real or imagined. Some of these efforts are really fine, others have little validity; some have only naïveté and fanciful invention, with no basis in fact and no standing in aesthetics. In their aggregate, however, there is a moving revelation of how potent a great man can become as a symbol; how the memory of a beloved leader can create its own legend in the hearts of a nation.

The examples are many, and in spite of a thorough search, the author knows that not all of them have been found. He has tried to gather together as wide a range of subjects as possible, from which to make the selection which follows.

Lee on the Field of Battle

The only known copy of this colored steel engraving has hung in the Confederate Museum, Richmond, as long as any living employee can remember. Rich in fanciful detail, it shows **Lee** in a black beaver instead of the regulation Confederate uniform hat. "Jeb" Stuart is in the background. The name of the artist and the date of execution are not known.

Lee at Fredericksburg

An oil painting by P. P. Carter, of Atlanta

A Meeting Not Historic: Lee, with Jackson and Johnston

This lithograph of an imagined conference is based on three distinct photographs. The head of "Stonewall" Jackson, left, is adapted from a photograph by Miley of Lexington. The face of Joseph E. Johnston, center, is shown as he was photographed more than a year after Jackson's death, shortly after Johnston was relieved of the command of the Army of Tennessee. Lee's head will be recognized as the Vannerson profile, dating from 1864, reproduced on page 41. That photograph also was taken after Jackson's death.

An Ideal Painting by Theodore Pine. 1904

Just Before Chancellorsville

The steel engraving shown opposite was widely published in the years following the war. It copies faithfully a painting by E. B. Fabrina Julio showing the last meeting of Lee and Jackson just before the great victory of Chancellorsville which ultimately cost "Stonewall" his life. Though it treats the terrain fancifully, the painter may have intended to depict the recorded moment, around seven o'clock on the morning of May 2, 1863, when Jackson, who was about to lead his entire corps into the forest for the surprise attack on Hooker's right flank, drew rein alongside Lee and spoke a few words that his staff could not hear.

The original painting, now in the Louisiana State Museum, was executed by Julio for the famed Washington Artillery of New Orleans. A replica by Julio hangs in the State Library at Baton Rouge.

A Portrait by Valentine

Obviously based on the photograph by Vannerson shown on page 45. As late as March of 1909, E. V. Valentine, then seventy-one, was still making portraits of the man whose face he had studied almost four decades earlier, a few months before death took Lee.

Oil Painting by M. S. Nagatries

The face seems to be derived from the Davies photograph (page 51), but the details of dress are borrowed from the Brady photographs after Appomattox.

A Portrait by J. A. Elder

This oil painting by a Richmond portraitist shows the influence of the photograph reproduced on page 82.

Another Portrait by J. A. Elder

The original is in the Corcoran Gallery, Washington

Two Idealized Paintings
in Richmond

The portrait at left is
in Battle Abbey.

The original of this painting is in the Westmoreland Club.

The Confederate General

Ernest L. Ipsen, who painted the fine reconstruction of Lee at West Point, shown on page 25, also created this idealized and highly spiritual conception of Lee as he was ten years later, in command of the Army of Northern Virginia. Executed for a private collection in Virginia.

Lee and His Generals

Imaginary group portraits of the Confederate generals in a landscape setting were popular after the war, bringing together assemblages which never existed in fact. This lithograph by Tholey is one of the early examples.

Summer

This impressive painting is one of a series of four large murals executed by Charles Hoffbauer in 1921 for the South Hall of the Confederate Memorial Institute, Richmond. Symbolizing the Confederate high command in the full summer of success, it offers an interesting contrast to the conception shown opposite. Here is the grand galaxy of figures, from "Jeb" Stuart at extreme right to Wade Hampton, astride at extreme left. General Lee is on Traveller.

In 1866, one year after Appomattox, two Philadelphia lithographers issued each his own wholly fanciful conception of the surrender, shown above and below. No such meetings took place.

CAPITULATION & SURRENDER OF ROBᵗ E. LEE & HIS ARMY AT APPOMATTOX CH. VA TO Lᵗ GENˡ U S GRANT
APRIL 9ᵗᴴ 1865

Twenty years later, the lithographers were still drawing on their imaginations. Equally false was this fantasy conceived in Chicago in 1885. It is true that on April 10, the day after the surrender in the McLean house, Lee and Grant met briefly on a knoll between the lines of the two armies. It was a half-hour visit of courtesy on the part of General Grant, and only a handful of staff officers were present.

Lee Surrenders at Appomattox

Alonzo Chappell in 1884 made this painting of the moment of Lee's signing on April 9, 1865. This is a wet-plate copy by Mathew Brady of the original painting; it became a popular illustration for many stories and historical accounts of the meeting.

Sunset After Appomattox

This fine oil portrait by Carl Gutherz, the creator of impressive murals in the Library of Congress, was destroyed by fire in Richmond many years ago, following an exhibition in the National Museum. It depicts Lee after reaction had set in following the meeting with Grant; the structure on the ridge is evidently intended to be the McLean house. Again there is no exact historical basis for an eloquent picture: on that afternoon, during which Lee was closely observed, no one noted that he ever sought solitude on the trunk of a fallen tree. Leaving the McLean house, he returned to the apple orchard from which he had sent his third note to Grant. Several hours were spent there pacing under a tree; near sunset he rode out to his headquarters, a mile to the rear.

A biographical sketch of Gutherz incorrectly credits him with an original portrait of Lee, based on a sitting in life. A Swiss-born immigrant to America, Gutherz gave up his work as a draughtsman in Memphis, Tenn., and went abroad for art instruction, returning at the age of 28 after extensive studies on the Continent. That was in 1872, two years after Lee's death.

The Surrender at Appomattox

Another conception of the surrender at the McLean house on April 9, 1865. This painting by B. West Clinedinst was made thirteen years after Chappell's painting, in 1897.

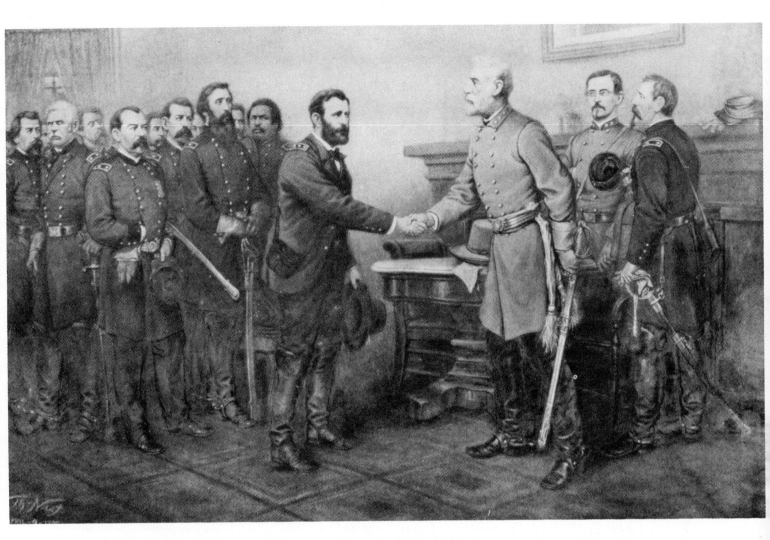

"Peace in Union"

The original of this painting, on a canvas nine by twelve feet, is on exhibition in the Museum of Galena, Illinois. It was executed by Thomas Nast on the commission of the late Herman H. Kohlsaat, of Chicago, who had been born in Galena.

The painting was brought to completion in Thomas Nast's studio in Morristown, New Jersey. Nast gave it the finishing touches on April 9, 1895, exactly thirty years after the day of the surrender, and eighteen days later it was unveiled in Galena, in ceremonies celebrating General Grant's birthday.

While Nast was at work on the painting in Morristown, he had as visitors several of the officers who had been present in the room with Lee and Grant, and he benefited by their criticism. Among them were Colonel Horace Porter, who is in the group of Union officers behind Grant, and Colonel Charles Marshall, Lee's aide, who stands directly behind the Confederate general. Colonel Marshall in particular showed a most active interest and was the source of many helpful corrections.

Thomas Nast's son, Cyril Nast, who was then sixteen years old, modelled for General Grant. He had on the jacket, boots, and field-glasses that Grant had worn on that memorable day; they had been lent for the purpose of the painting by Frederick Dent Grant, a son. Cyril Nast recalls that his father had been reluctant to mass all the Federal officers directly behind Grant, believing that some of them would have entered the room singly and unobtrusively. He had deferred, however, to the wish of Kohlsaat, who wanted those officers pictured in a compact group of portraits. The physical details of room and furniture were based on painstaking research.

Three Scenes Out of Lee's Day at Appomattox

Above is a drawing by W. Taber, based on a lithograph by W. H. Stelle, "The Dawn of Peace," which apparently has not survived.

A. R. Waud's "sketch made at the time" shows General Lee and Colonel Marshall leaving the McLean house after the surrender.

W. L. Sheppard's war-time sketch, executed here by M. Jones as an engraving on wood, depicts General Lee's return to his lines following the surrender.

An "Artistic Novelty"

The famous New York firm of Currier and Ives, "Print makers to the American People," took pride in their artistic novelties. Published here for the first time is this "three-way" print showing three of the Confederacy's leaders. Viewing it directly from the front, one sees the picture of Jefferson Davis; at a forty-five-degree angle to the left, the picture of "Stonewall" Jackson appears; the same angle from the right shows Robert E. Lee. The lithograph of Lee is a rendering in reverse of the engraving by A. Robin reproduced on page 33.

Lee at the Grave of Jackson

Lee's admiring affection for "Stonewall" Jackson, who was buried in Lexington, Lee's home after the war, made a highly romantic appeal to the imagination of the artist, as evidenced by this colored lithograph by Volck (1872).

In the colored lithograph shown opposite, the conception of another artist, every detail is different, and Lee in face and figure seems to step straight out of the Brady photographs taken on the back porch in Richmond in the spring of 1865.

Lee as President of Washington College

George P. A. Healy (1813-1894), who achieved some distinction as a painter of portraits, made this posthumous study, apparently from photograph sources easily traced in this book. It is in the collection of Mrs. C. H. Besly, of Hinsdale, Illinois.

J. A. Elder, two of whose hypothetical portraits of Lee in his military career have been shown on pages 112 and 113, made another study of Lee as he might have looked as President of Washington College. It is evident that one photograph (page 82) was the main inspiration for all three paintings. The painting shown above was owned by the late Dr. George Bolling Lee.

Two Outstanding Portraits of the College President

Above: This fine portrait by John Dabour, Smyrna-born portraitist, may yet be proved to have been done from life. Despite Dabour's active career in portraiture, the record of his life is extremely meager. Apparently he came to the United States in 1867, three years before Lee died. No record of a sitting exists, though there is a possibility that the painting was made in Baltimore in the ten days of Lee's stay there in the spring of 1869. Carrying all of the conviction of an original, it is not traceable to photographs. This portrait is in the collection of Mr. Walter H. Taylor.

On the facing page is a notable portrait executed by Hattie E. Burdette of Washington, D. C. on the inspiration of Miley photographs. It now hangs in the office of Dr. Francis P. Gaines, president of Washington and Lee University.

Lee in his Study at Washington College

This large colored lithograph by A. J. Volck, executed in 1873, three years after Lee's death, was circulated widely throughout the South. The details of the room are accurate. Lee's office in the basement of the College chapel remains today exactly as it was when he last walked out of it on the afternoon of September 28, 1870.

"Lee in the Mountains"

This impressionistic study finds its mystical inspiration in part in the moving photograph on page 99. Painted in 1936 by Mr. Avery Handley Jr. of Winchester, Tennessee, for Mr. Donald Davidson of Vanderbilt University, it is now in the latter's collection. "The content of the painting," the artist says in explanation, "issued from a dark and massive background of emotions, romantic fevers and facts which suddenly became activated into an object or image under the impact of an elegiac poem by Mr. Davidson entitled 'Lee in the Mountains.' . . . I believe the concrete image which is seen in one blow, as it were, more serviceable a point upon which to base an attitude perhaps than a form requiring a sequence of time."

Reduced to the monochrome of a photograph, the character of the painting is not lost, the artist feels, since it is chiefly composed of brown and white values with accents of yellow and pale green.

After executing this portrait, Mr. Handley saw service in World War II. "I found myself staring into the jovian face of Lee and receiving courage in situations which arose at times when I was on active duty in the Navy," he writes.

In the State Capitol, Richmond, is this statue by Rudulph Evans, placed there in 1931. On the day which it commemorates, Lee's manly bearing made a deep impression on all beholders. To have portrayed him in any other way than as the bearded military figure who became the epitome of Southern resistance would have beclouded the symbol; but it is one of the lesser ironies of history that when the new Major General stood before the Virginia convention he did not look like this. He wore a moustache but no beard, and was presumably in civilian attire.

In Statuary Hall, Washington, D. C., stands this gift from the State of Virginia—a bronze figure executed by Edward V. Valentine, who had studied Lee in life with the eye of the sculptor.

In 1872, William R. O'Donovan, a Virginian and a Confederate veteran, modeled this plaque and presented it to the Virginia State Library. Self-taught in sculpture, O'Donovan had many important sitters in portraiture and fashioned several outstanding public monuments, such as the lifesize equestrian high-reliefs of Grant and Lincoln which were placed in 1894 on the piers of the Soldiers' and Sailors' Memorial Arch in Prospect Park Plaza, Brooklyn.

The late George T. Brewster, who was born in 1862, the year that brought the first of General Lee's great military triumphs, created the bust which stands in New York University's Hall of Fame.

In Lee Park, at Charlottesville, stands this equestrian statue, erected in 1937 through funds provided by Alexander Wilbourne Weddell, president of the Virginia Historical Society, and Mrs. Weddell. Henry M. Shrady, originally commissioned as sculptor, died after his cast model had been approved. The statue was executed with modifications by Leo Lentelli.

The cast model of the Lee equestrian statue on the Virginia Memorial at Gettysburg National Park, by Frederick William Sievers, as photographed in 1910 by Huestis Cook, whose father, George Cook, was a famous Confederate photographer.

Prominent in Dallas, Texas, is this finely spirited equestrian group of Lee and a young soldier, the work of A. Phimister Proctor. It stands admirably placed in Lee Park.

"THE LAST REVIEW"

ON THE TWENTY-NINTH OF MAY, 1890, came the unveiling in Richmond of the heroic statue of Lee on Traveller which writes finis to this pictorial record of his Legend. Three years earlier the commission had been given to the distinguished French sculptor, Marius Jean Antonin Mercié, who had done, among other outstanding works, a monument of King Louis Philippe and Queen Amélie for their tomb at Dreux.

The unveiling was a great moment in the living tradition of the Confederacy. Robert E. Lee had been dead for twenty years, but there was a notable coming together of the Confederate great to do him honor. What would have pleased him most was the army of thousands of veterans—a middle-aged army now: infantrymen, cavalrymen, artillerymen—who passed in review before their revered commander. Some of the lieutenants in whom he put his deepest trust were still at hand—Generals John B. Gordon, James Longstreet, Wade Hampton, Fitzhugh Lee, Harry Heth, E. P. Alexander, Jubal A. Early, Joseph E. Johnston. There were two widows of distinguished Confederates: Mrs. Thomas J. Jackson and Mrs. George E. Pickett. Three of Lee's children were there.

The pull on the rope that brought the veiling down from around the monument came from the hand of General Joseph E. Johnston. He was then eighty-three, and he died the next year.

NEW ILLUSTRATIONS FOR THE 1981 EDITION

Since the first publication of *The Face of Robert E. Lee* in 1947, I have discovered some interesting pictures of the distinguished confederate soldier. Tracing the origins of old paintings and photographs is somewhat like being a detective, but in the case of the illustrations in the following pages the task wasn't too difficult.

The following five artistic compositions are from the United States Military Academy's West Point Collections, and the Museum of the Confederacy at Richmond, Virginia.

The first is an oil portrait by G. Louvrie. Believed to have been painted sometime in the 1848-1853 period, the painting depicts Lee at 45, when he was a Captain (Brevet Colonel)* United States Army Corps of Engineers, and Superintendent of the Military Academy at West Point. Lee is dressed immaculately in the same civilian clothes he wore for the daguerreotype made by Mathew B. Brady in the latter's new Washington gallery in 1848. The only difference is the artist's deletion of the hands, gloves, and high hat.

The second is a carefully-drawn pen and ink sketch of a cadet cap by Colonel Lee, when Superintendent of the Academy. The drawing is rare and believed to be previously unpublished. Drawing and map-making were mandatory at the Academy. I am indebted to Michael E. Moss, Curator of Art, West Point Museum, for calling my attention to this interesting drawing.

Sidney Edward Dickinson's three-quarter length oil portrait of General Lee was made in 1951. Copied from a full-length photograph taken by Mathew B. Brady in Richmond in April of 1865, the painting is faithful, but the artist replaced the original background with an allegorical one. Mr. Dickinson, a student of William Merritt Chase at the National Academy, was born in 1890. He died on May 4, 1980, at the age of ninety.

Harry A. Ogden, author of the delightful watercolor of General Lee on Traveller, was a nineteenth-century artist, famous for his military paintings. His watercolor is faithful to the Miley photograph made in Richmond.

Lastly, the stylized pen and ink drawing heightened in white chalk, or designer's white, shows Lee in camp wearing jackboots, sword, field glasses, and sash. In all probability, the artist made his drawing from the Minnis and Cowell photograph shown on page 39.

---

*A brevet commission bestows higher rank without higher pay. The job of Superintendent of the Academy called for a colonelcy.

Captain (Brevet Colonel) Robert Edward Lee (1852-1853)

Lee out of uniform, as he looked when Superintendent of the United States Military Academy at West Point. Painted by G. Louvrie, who undoubtedly used Mathew B. Brady's first daguerreo-type made in Washington, D. C., when Brady opened his first gallery there.

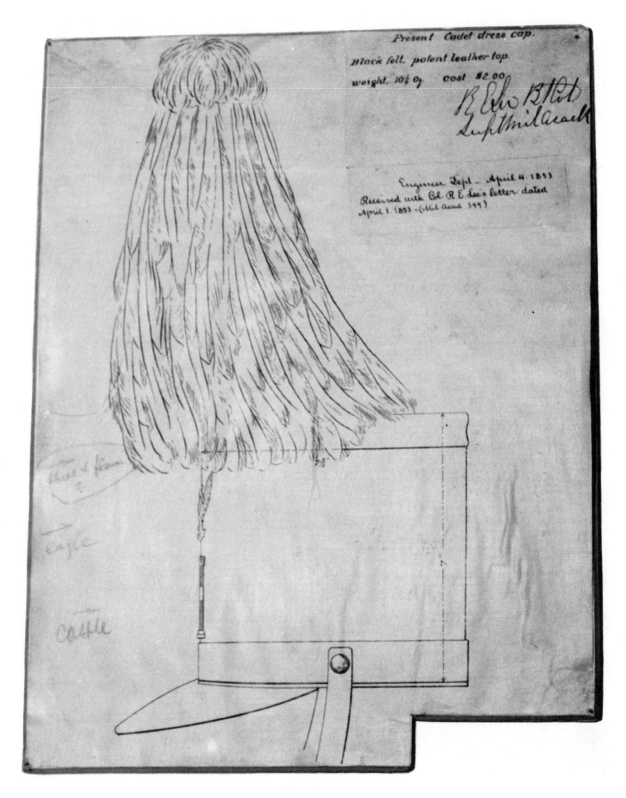

Colonel Robert E. Lee's Drawing of a Cadet Cap (ca. 1853)

Signed Robert E. Lee, "Bvt. Col. Superintendent," this pen and ink drawing of "Present Cadet Dress Cap," describes it as being of "Black felt, with patent leather top. Weight 10¼ ounces. Cost $2.00." The drawing is dated April 4, 1853.

General Robert E. Lee in 1865

Lee as he looked in 1865, shortly after the surrender at Appomattox in April. Sidney Edward Dickinson painted the picture in 1951 and used Mathew B. Brady's photograph as the model. The allegorical background was added.

General Robert E. Lee in Watercolor

Harry A. Ogden, well-known nineteenth-century painter of military scenes, made this original watercolor of Lee on Traveller, his favorite war horse. Somewhat romanticized, it shows Lee as he looks in the Miley photograph. The date of the painting is unknown.

General Lee in Camp

This meticulous engraving, in all probability, was executed from the Minnis and Cowell photograph made in Richmond during the war (see page 39). The background has been completely stylized, with war clouds and all accoutrements with the uniform. The artist is unknown.

B
Lee
Meredith
The face of Robert E. Lee in
   life and in legend